M. A. Stephens,
Montreal,
1943.

TOWARDS A CHRISTIAN ORDER

TOWARDS
A CHRISTIAN ORDER

by

THE BISHOP OF CHELMSFORD
THE REV. CANON S. J. MARRIOTT
THE REV. CANON A. E. BAKER
THE REV. W. G. PECK   THE REV. F. C. POND
SIR RICHARD ACLAND, M.P.
THE HEADMASTER OF RUGBY
RUTH KENYON   A. TRYSTAN EDWARDS
SIDNEY DARK

With an Introduction by
THE
ARCHBISHOP OF CANTERBURY

LONDON
EYRE & SPOTTISWOODE, LTD.
14, 15 & 16 BEDFORD STREET
W.C. 2

First Published . . . 1942

THIS BOOK IS PRODUCED IN
COMPLETE CONFORMITY WITH THE
AUTHORIZED ECONOMY STANDARDS

PRINTED IN GREAT BRITAIN FOR
EYRE AND SPOTTISWOODE (PUBLISHERS) LIMITED, LONDON

CONTENTS

EDITORS' NOTE

THE essays in this volume are suggested by the Findings of the Malvern Conference, the outstanding importance of which is now generally recognised. President Roosevelt recently said: "We plan now for the better world we aim to build." Sir John Orr has written in his latest book: "It should now be clear to everybody that the old world order is passing away. The economic and political structure, built on the Industrial Revolution, is like a house being gutted by fire. To talk of economic reconstruction in the sense of merely repairing the damage caused by the war is to talk nonsense."

It is, therefore, of immense concern to all Christians to have some clear idea of the qualities of the "better world" for which they are praying. Accordingly the contributors to this volume, each from his own point of view, have considered the fundamental evils of the old order and the essential characteristics of any Christian order, with practical and, in some cases, differing suggestions as to how that order may be secured.

It should be repeated that each writer is alone responsible for what he has written. The Editorial Committee—the Lord Bishop of Bradford, the Lord Bishop of Chelmsford, the Rev. P. T. R. Kirk and Sidney Dark—is responsible for the selection of the subjects, all of them suggested by the Malvern Findings, and for the invitations to the various contributors.

INTRODUCTION

By The Archbishop of Canterbury

As I was responsible for inviting the "Malvern Conference" to assemble and also in large measure for the form of the propositions which it accepted as its "Findings," it is natural that I should be asked to supply an Introduction to this volume in which many of the principles briefly stated in those "Findings" are worked out more fully in relation to the actual situation to-day.

The "Findings" of the Malvern Conference have been very widely discussed. There was little, if anything, in them which had not been said repeatedly before by such leaders of Christian social thought as Bishop Gore and Canon Scott Holland. But the re-publication of those principles early in 1941 found a public ready to attend to them with a new eagerness.

If left undeveloped, the Malvern "Findings" could have little value. They need to be worked out. They are, I believe, a useful starting point; but they are no more than a starting point. In this volume ways of working them out are offered which may assist still further the development of a thoughtful public opinion, ready to influence our action as a nation now, and, still more, when the time for post-war reconstruction comes. That at that time such a public opinion should exist and assert itself is of the greatest importance.

The first of the following essays contains a quotation from "a recent issue of the *Tribune*":

"Every Sunday and several times a week the B.B.C. tells the world that we are fighting for Christianity."

I wonder whether, in fact, the writer of that sentence has ever heard this said at all. Certainly I have not. It would be a wrong thing to say, because (as the writer rather scornfully explains) it is not true; but also it would be a wrong thing to do. You must never fight—physically—for Christianity, because you can always serve it better by another method, namely, martyrdom. Moreover, Christianity exists only where it is freely accepted; the use of force on behalf of it is therefore a betrayal of it.

But while this is true of Christianity itself, it does not follow that it is also true of a civilisation largely influenced by Christianity and threatened by one which has deliberately repudiated the fundamental elements in the Christian conception of life and the way to live. We are fighting to preserve a civilisation that has never, of course, been completely Christian, but has been

8

very deeply influenced by the Christian view of life; and we are fighting to keep open the possibility of a still more truly Christian civilisation in the future.

No doubt many of those who fight would by no means recognise that description of their purpose. Christianity has not—to our shame—been presented to them in such a way as might enable them to recognise it as the source and inspiration of what they value. So the formulation of our purpose has to be translated for them into such terms as Justice, Freedom, Truth, and the like.

But if we are fighting to win for the world a fuller expression of Justice, Freedom, and Truth in the life of men, we must not only defeat the forces which despise these great qualities, but must secure that they actually prevail to a greater extent than before in the world of the future. This will require thought, courage, and readiness—in the more privileged at least—for sacrifice. The writers of the following essays will help towards that sincere thinking without which courage and self-sacrifice will be unavailing.

They do not all agree; and I do not agree with all of them. As regards the closing essays, where provision is deliberately made for the expression of different views, I should like to express my own conviction that no one type of organisation is likely to be the best for every sort of enterprise. In some cases "nationalisation" may be the best solution, in others "national guilds." In others again something more like the individual enterprise with which we are more familiar. No doubt the example of the Public Utility Corporations will be widely followed. The vital matter is that in all cases the public interest should be recognised as supreme over the interest of individuals or groups.

But no form of organisation can save men from sin; and sinful men will pervert any form of organisation. Common ownership can be quite as bad as private ownership; it can, I think, be worse. Acquisitiveness can fasten on power as readily as upon wealth—indeed, it is for the sake of power that most men desire wealth. Christianity has much to say about the right ordering of life, and more ought to be heard of this than has been heard for some centuries; but it has still more to say about the kind of character needed by those who are to work whatever system is established—and the more Christian the system the more thoroughly Christian must be those who work it if it is not to break down—and also about the ways in which that character may be acquired and developed. That is not the subject of this book; but unless it is mentioned here, what follows may be seen in a false perspective.

WILLIAM CANTUAR:

August 31, 1942

THE CHRISTIAN ORDER

The Malvern Findings are prefaced by the declaration: "The first, and if fully understood, the whole duty of the Church is truly to be the Church—the community of the Holy Spirit drawing men and nations into itself, that they may become sharers in its God-given life and so fulfil their several destinies according to God's purpose." It has, therefore, been appropriate to print as the first essay in this volume Canon Marriott's warning of the danger that, with its renewed conviction that it must use all its spiritual influence to help this generation "to find the plan whereby economic justice and international harmony may be established," the Church may neglect its paramount duty to proclaim that personal "holiness is not only that without which no man shall see the Lord, it is also that without which no man can do His work."

Canon Marriott, obviously influenced by Berdyaev, is fearful that the righteous revolt against social abuses may result in comparative indifference to personal religion. He recalls that men like Lowder and Dolling were "aflame for social righteousness but the flame was one which was taken from the altar and tended in the silence of daily meditation" and the motif of his essay is to be found in the assertion that "our social evils are becoming a most useful whipping-post for our private sins."

The essay is provocative. Some of the assertions such as that Marxism must be radically anti-Christian would have been accepted by Lenin but will certainly be hotly denied by many Christian thinkers. But it is of vital importance that, in thinking of a Christian order, it should be made clear that it is an order of human life guided and inspired by the Holy Spirit.

THE CHRISTIAN ORDER

THE SOUL OF MAN

By S. J. Marriott, Canon of Westminster

"Quo vadis?" "Whither goest thou?" To ask that of our present world is to be reminded vividly of the chaos and confusion in which we live, and therefore of the rashness of any man who would attempt to foretell the shape of things to come. But on one point there seems to be increasing agreement, namely, that the basic meaning of these turbulent days is that an old world, alias "*modern times*," has come to an end, and that a new one is struggling to be born. On the lips of political leaders the world over the word "new" is continually heard. Hitler has his "New Order," Roosevelt his "New Deal," we our "New World after the war." But are they new, or only attempts to maintain or renovate the old?

The vast inequalities of wealth, the widespread unemployment, the ever-increasing social and international unrest which marked the years between the two World Wars, showed that the social cohesion of our civilisation was giving way, as when the bastion of some old castle is imperilled because the mortar between the bricks has crumbled.

It is possible to prolong the life of such a bastion by girding it round with an iron band. Such is the rationale of Fascism. It is an attempt to hold together by force a civilisation which in itself is dissolving. The Dictator and the Gestapo represent an attempt to hold back the oncoming tide of history, but it will obey the bidding of Hitler as little as it did that of King Canute.

But is the "new world after the war" of which the democracies speak to be really new or only a renovation of the old? Certainly Capitalism is doomed, but Socialism, according to Berdyaev, is only Capitalism in a new guise. "Socialists take over from bourgeois society," he writes, "its capitalism, its atheism, its cheap prophets, its hostility to the spirit and all spiritual life, its restless striving for success and amusement, its personal selfishness."[1] That is an exaggeration, perhaps, yet in so far as socialism seeks to distribute money more fairly but still regards the money-factor as the keynote of man's life, it will not lead to a new world, but to a different version of the old. Newness is only possible if man accepts a new scale of values, a new philosophy of life, a new

[1] Berdyaev, *The End of Our Era.*

conception of the future. Anything less will in the long run prove
illusory if, in the turmoil and upheaval of these days, a new
world is in fact struggling to birth. Such occasions are very rare
in history, for though history is a story of continual change and
development, yet for the most part it shows us the working-out
of some basic idea on which the civilisation of a period rests,
usually extending for some centuries. But at rare and distant
intervals the theme of history changes; it takes a completely new
direction. It was so when the Roman Empire fell and was
replaced eventually by Feudal Europe: and again when Feudal
Europe came to an end with the Reformation, out of which our
modern world was born. In each case continuity is not lost, one
merges into the other: yet Roman Imperialism, Mediaeval
Feudalism, and Modern Industrialism are different in their
themes. It is at such a fatal juncture that our world stands to-day:
but what will be the shape of things to come? Everything points
to a great socialization in the life of man, both nationally and
internationally, but it may well prove that more than socialism,
as we understand it to-day, will be required to effect it. Berdyaev's
statement which I have quoted needs qualifying because he seems
to regard socialism and communism as identical, while in this
country we have a tradition of socialism which is ethical and has
its roots in Christian teaching, not in the Marxian dialectic.
Nevertheless his words contain a warning, and one which should
be borne in mind by those who abandon themselves too un-
critically to the cry for "Socialism in our Day".

Here, for example, is a paragraph taken from a recent issue
of the *Tribune*:

> Every Sunday and several times a week the B.B.C. tells the world
> that we are fighting for Christianity. Who says so? Certainly not
> the people who are doing the fighting. Are the Russians fighting
> for Christianity? Are the Jews fighting for Christianity? Are our
> own men fighting for Christianity? The boys in the Commando
> and parachute regiments—did they volunteer for the job because
> they are devout Christians? The boys who flew to bomb Augsburg
> in daylight, knowing that they would never come back—were they
> inspired by the vague miasma which is called the Christian way of
> life? Like hell.

One can see a half-truth in what the writer says, but the
significant thing is the spirit in which the words are written. It
would be folly to ignore the fact that that spirit is not uncommon,
and that a revolution in this country also may be atheistic as
well as socialistic. That is the warning which Berdyaev would
have us bear in mind.

In a letter to me recently an author, well known for his books on social and economic subjects, wrote, "To see Christianity with the eyes of an honest and intelligent Bolshevik is, I think, one of the most salutary experiences for a Christian. It involves a deep moral repugnance to religion which is startling." I am sure it does. But a "deep moral repugnance to religion" only is a euphemism for a violent hatred of God. For if there is no God there is no religion, and I doubt whether that passion can be called "moral", even though it is most salutary for a Christian to realise that that is what he is up against.

Nevertheless there is in this country a socialism to which people are attracted because they see in it, not the destruction of Christianity, but at least its partial realisation.

Does not the greed and self-seeking implicit in the profit-motive on which Capitalism rests flout the whole substance of Christ's teaching? How can His teaching on the brotherhood of man and on the equal value of every man in the sight of God be realised in a social order productive of such gross inequalities and injustices that bitterness and class-war become inevitable? Such are the questions they ask, and not only ask, but feel strongly about, and that is why they throw themselves so keenly into the struggle for a new social order.

It is not only those who have experienced the effects of long periods of unemployment who are determined that it shall not be permitted to recur again after the war. One of the most promising signs in the country is this steady growth of a determined, militant Christianity. Thousands of people, on sincerely Christian grounds, will not rest content until they see put into effect their demand for a more just and Christian order in our national affairs.

And they are right, so right that neither the assertion that religion has nothing to do with political and economic questions, nor the extent of the changes which a truly Christian social order may demand, should deter them.

But this presents the Church with the intensely difficult task of finding the *via media* between an "other-worldly" religion, which confines itself to the problems of the soul and ignores the problems of the street, and a "this-worldly" religion which is so concerned with the social problems of its day that its contact with the spiritual world is wearing very thin.

And mark you, that very term *"via media"* is more than suspect to-day, it is violently disliked. To the political socialist it means being "pink", and the pink socialist is to him a timid reformer who lacks the guts to go out for "socialism in our time". To the ardent Christian communist within the Church it means the typical "hedging" parson, who is not going to commit himself to socialism till he is quite sure that socialism is going to win.

In that connection it may help us to remember that in the case of Jesus the "*via media*" turned out to be the "*via crucis*". In overturning the tables of the money-changers He protested against the exploitation of the people for monetary ends. He attacked what was the stronghold of capitalism in His day; and that act was more instrumental in bringing about His death than is usually recognised. Annas was the most powerful man in Jerusalem, able to wield that political influence which high finance has wielded in this country for so long. On the other hand, when the mob was asked to choose between Barabbas and Jesus it did not hesitate in its choice. There before them on the balcony stood the two figures, the brawny, die-hard Barabbas who had led an insurrection against the hated Romans, and would lead another if he got the chance; and the pale, bloodstained prophet from Nazareth. That He was very kind to the poor, possessed wonderful powers to heal the sick and spoke beautiful things, was undeniable, but if it came to the job of turning out their hated masters, He was not the man for it. "Come unto me all ye that travail and are heavy laden" was all very well, but the cry of Barabbas, "Come unto me all ye that are strong and will fight to the death," was more to the point. For the real work of the world it is not revivalists that are wanted but revolutionaries, "reds" not "pinks".

And let us remember that though the Passion and Crucifixion of Jesus took place at a certain historical point in time yet the drama of Calvary is in its nature eternal, and for that reason it is always present in history. While therefore it is possible that the Church may be reinstated in popular favour by interesting itself in the social and economic problems of the day, it may also go to the Cross if its witness to the truth in these matters is faithful. He would be a rash man who would assert categorically whether in the not distant future the Church will be the Church of the Catacombs or the Church of the People.

But though the task before the Church to-day is a very delicate one it has the Light of the World to guide it; and all that matters is that we be true to that Light irrespective of consequences. "It is required of a steward that he be found faithful," and for that reason our primary task is not to discover the right solution of our economic troubles, but the right attitude towards them—and by "right" we mean that which Christ would have us adopt. On that matter also there will be difference of opinion, but not, I think, as regards one basic principle which He makes clear. To arrive at it I would venture to use a parable that was in fact a miracle; namely, the Feeding of the Five Thousand. There we see Jesus dealing with the economic problem; for the economic problem is at heart the problem of the people's bread and how to make it go round. Now if the individuals who handed over the few loaves and fishes had explained that though they were prepared to share these with the crowd, nevertheless they would, as owners, expect to receive a larger share, you would have a rudimentary example of capitalism, of an economic based on ownership. "Because we own the capital we are entitled to a larger share of the proceeds."

If the crowd had become angry at this claim and demanded that all should share and share alike, even though it meant but a few crumbs for each, and that it would be a bad day for the "owners" if they did not consent, the result would have been the communist economic. Private ownership is disallowed: all things belong to the people.

While, further, if some strong individual had got one or two like-minded men round him and explained to them that the way to solve the difficulty was for them to enforce their will on owners and crowd alike, and made it clear to both parties that it would be very much the worse for them if they did not do as they were told, one would arrive at Nazi economics. Under that system the economic problem, like all others, is solved by the Gestapo.

But what is certain is that under each and all of these systems what results is bitterness, bloodshed, broken heads, and broken hearts; and in no case does the bread go round.

How Jesus performed that miracle is beyond our knowing, but it is significant that He preached to the crowd before He fed them. For two days He put before them "the bread that cometh down from Heaven" before He attempted to feed them with the bread that cometh up from the earth. What difference did that make? Only this, that by the time you had listened to Jesus talking and become subject to His influence, your desire was not to get all you could but to share what you had. If it is love that makes the world go round, it is likewise only love that makes the bread go round.

It sounds platitudinous, perhaps it is; but it confronts our troubled world with an inexorable law, namely, this, that *economic troubles can only be cured by transcending the economic motive.* So long as the acquisitive motive, the profit motive, is predominant, nothing but strife and division can ensue, because they are implicit in the motive itself.

Vast inequalities of wealth, unemployment, class strife, and international war are not aberrations of our economic system, they are inherent in it. For that reason no solution of our economic troubles can be found so long as our attention is confined only to the economic sphere. Neither capitalism, communism,

not socialism can provide it because each in different degrees is
infected with the same evil in that it accepts the economic motive
as supreme in the life of man. But in the teaching of Jesus that
motive is itself the very evil which has to be cured.

How inevitable it is that Marxism is, and must be, radically
anti-Christian! To Karl Marx it is not a hypothesis but an axiom
that the life of man is governed by the economic motive: to Jesus
it was equally axiomatic that "man shall not live by bread alone".
The gospel of the former is "seek ye first the right distribution
of wealth and the Kingdom of Man shall be added unto you";
the gospel of the latter is "Seek ye first the Kingdom of God and
His justice and these things (food and clothing) shall be added
unto you". To the one salvation lies only in the economic sphere,
to the other it lies only in transcending the economic motive
altogether. Nor is this by any means irrelevant to our subject,
since we are being deluged with plans, programmes, and blue-
prints by individuals and parties of all descriptions. They differ
as much as black from white but all are alike in this that they
take for granted that the way through our troubles, the way into
the "new world after the war", lies in finding the right plan,
which each professes to have found. That is to say, each sees
salvation in the right technique, which is perfectly natural in an
age governed by technics. Each sees it in an external change in
man's environment, not in an internal change in man himself;
and in that respect each, even the most die-hard defender of
Right Wing politics, is a disciple of Karl Marx, not of Jesus of
Nazareth. To every problem there are two sides, the problem of
the plan and the problem of the man, the technical and the human.
It was instinctive to Jesus to put the human first. In the miracle
we have just considered, His first act was to put the crowd into
the right disposition by His preaching. By inducing in them the
desire to share, He produced the best possible conditions for
dealing with the economic situation. He put the man first, and
the plan second. Our world-improvers of to-day reverse that order.

It is not a question of either . . . or, but of priority. Most
certainly the plan must be found; it would be dangerous and
culpable reaction if the Church to-day were to confine itself to
the preaching of individual piety and ignore the burning social
problems around which the actual history of our day is revolving.
If nature abhors a vacuum, no less does religion. Christianity
rests on the doctrine of the Incarnation and its social objective
is to incarnate in the sphere of the temporal (i.e. in the social,
political, and economic field) the eternal values of the spiritual
world. "The Word became Flesh"; it must always become flesh.
To avoid the stern struggle to which that calls us by resorting

to a "purely spiritual" religion is sheer escapism, as much as was the attitude of the Priest and Levite when they "passed by on the other side". Whether we like the fact or not the Church to-day must do its utmost to help our generation find the "plan" whereby economic justice and international harmony can be established. Or, rather, it must do its utmost to produce from its ranks the Christian economists, Christian political and social reformers who by their expert knowledge and first-hand experience in the matters under dispute are qualified to do so. But in saying that, we have admitted that the primary duty of the Church is to provide the right man, not the right plan.

If that is a platitude it is one to which our enemies paid marked respect. Hitler was well aware that his first and paramount duty was to produce the Nazi man. That done, the revolutionising of the life of Germany according to the Nazi plan was plain sailing. Then why are the social reformers and world-improvers in the democracies entirely concerned with programmes and blue-prints, and singularly blind to the necessity of producing the type of man who will implement them? "The children of this world are in their generation wiser than the children of light." The myth of Nordic man and the purity of German blood may be nonsense, and probably is. But that is a matter of no consequence whatever. Blood, race, and soil belong to the organic, economics to the inorganic. You cannot derive life from the non-living, and for that reason Hitler never attempted to revitalise Germany by a new economic, but by producing new Germans. So, likewise, communism is not a new economic, but the communist is a new type of man. His communism is a passion in his whole being, not merely an economic theory in his brain. Then why in this country do we expend our energies on plans, plans, plans, dealing entirely with the technical and ignoring the human, indulging in the delusive hope that we can build a new world simply by drawing up a new plan?

It cannot be done. The heart of economics, the heart of politics, the heart of all social problems is the human heart. It is perfectly right that the Church should concern itself with the problems of a Christian Social Order; it is perfectly wrong that it should turn a blind eye to the fact that the Christians necessary to build it are steadily diminishing in numbers. In that connection Dr. Kennedy issues a timely warning when he writes:

> The modern idolatry of structure and organisation may clothe itself in imposing words and social ritual, but it covers the spiritual bankruptcy of the modern man, and is increasingly failing to satisfy his desire to be identified with something which is morally creative...[1]

---

[1] Dr. J. Kennedy, *Towards a Theocracy.*

Is there no danger that preoccupation with the Christian Social Order may also hide the spiritual bankruptcy of the modern Church? Speak to an audience of soldiers or of working-men of "the new world after the war" in terms of economic justice and equality of opportunity, attained by the application of Christian principles to national affairs, and they will listen. Speak to them about the life of prayer and faith, about the inner religiousness which is the very heart of the Christian religion, and their interest flags. Why? Partly because inner religiousness has no economic value, but also because social preaching implies that sin does not lie in them, but in the structure of society. Under the Christian flag they can fight for a better world without the necessity of themselves having to become better men. Very comforting, but very untrue! Our social evils are becoming a most useful whipping-post for our private sins. Again it is a question of priority, and we should note that though the Church to-day is competent in sociology, is more intellectually wide-awake on social problems than perhaps it has ever been, yet not for a century has it been so impotent in the sphere of evangelism. Perhaps a turn of the tide can be seen in the "Religion and Life" weeks, which certainly appear to be the right form of evangelism for present conditions.

The right attitude therefore of the Church towards the vexed social and economic troubles of our day is not only to take a deeply human interest in them, because they affect so vitally the lives of our people and the future of mankind, and to contribute everything that it can towards the finding of a right solution, but it must at the same time aver repeatedly that the solution cannot be found within the technical field alone. It must warn people that the "new world after the war" will go exactly the same way as did the "land fit for heroes to live in", that its vision of a social order in which injustice and unemployment have been replaced by equality of opportunity and security of work will prove a mirage if they are left to the politician, the economist, the socialist, the business organiser alone. They may become irritated when we tell them that religion alone can supply the vision and the will to build the city of their dreams, but we must say it and say it again because it is true.

Early in the Bible we read of a vaunting humanism which, confident in its own powers, said, "Go to, let us build us a city and a tower whose top may reach unto the heaven, and let us make us a name". The result was Babel, and all through the Bible, Babylon stands as the symbol of world empire, rich and powerful, but also cruel and unbelieving. But Babylon is always falling, empires crash and civilisations perish. That is the story of the world cities which man builds.

On the other hand, at the end of the Bible and in contrast with Babylon we read of the New Jerusalem, the holy city; but St. John records that he saw it "coming down out of Heaven from God". "Let us build up . . ." "I saw it coming down . . ." Our world needs much to be reminded of these two opposing ways of world building, lest it erect a new city after the war and omit the cement of religion which alone keeps its walls together.

Stated in this way the idea may sound fanciful, but thoughtful economists and historians are saying the same thing to-day in their own language. In his recent book, *Conditions of Peace*, Professor Carr writes:

> The position which we have reached to-day is that we no longer believe in amelioration by the automatic process of the pursuit of self-interest, that we recognise that progress can be achieved only by deliberate planning, but that we continue to ignore the problem of the moral purpose. . . . The months immediately after the war will be fully as critical and as hazardous for Great Britain and for the world as were the summer months of 1940. The essential nature of the crisis through which we are living is neither military, nor political, nor economic, but moral. A new faith in a new moral purpose is required to re-animate our political and economic system.

What is that but to say that we can only cure our economic troubles by learning to transcend the economic motive? The right moral purpose is the first desideratum if the right economic is to be found. He goes further when he writes:

> It is not inconceivable that the new leadership for which the world craves may arise from within the Christian Church. But this hypothesis appears to resuppose a transformation of Christianity, or a revival of its primitive spirit, which would in itself amount to a revolution.

In writing that he echoes the thoughts of many hearts. The very people who cannot imagine any leadership coming from the Church as it stands, have nevertheless an instinctive conviction that the vision and motive power necessary to build a happier world of the future are hidden in the Christian religion, and in the Christian religion alone. But they are equally convinced that nothing less than a revolution in the Church would ever make Christianity an effective force again in the life of the nation. Perhaps one danger in the Church devoting so much time to the reforms needed in the national life is that thereby its attention is distracted from the revolution needed in its own.

Another witness to the truth that we must rise above the economic plane if we would solve our economic troubles is Mr. Peter Drucker. Looking upon our blitzed and battered world of to-day he sees the significance of all its bloodshed, turmoil, and confusion as "The End of Economic Man". It is not just a fight against a demonic Führer, it is not just a contest between democracy and dictatorship, it is the end of an age which has regarded the economic motive as supreme in the life of man. No tinkering with our economic system, no attempt to find a working compromise between capitalism and socialism will suffice, man needs to be delivered from that servitude to money and the machine which has brought Western civilisation to its present pass.

There is a pathetic yet passionate yearning in the heart of man to-day for a human world, because his economic world has issued in the most devilish inhumanism. There is something demonic in the rule of money and the machine and man has sensed it. It was that yearning which produced such a heartfelt response to the recent speech of the American Vice-President. He said that the peace after this war must be a people's peace, the world after this war a people's world. Listeners knew he was not thinking of the proletariat, of the mass, of the mob; he was saying what they longed to hear, that in the world after the war man's longing for freedom, for fellowship, for right relationships with his neighbour shall take precedence of all other problems. But for that the reordering of the economic world is not enough, nothing less that its dethronement will do. It is not a question of reducing profits and increasing wages, of levelling up or levelling down, but of making the whole world of finance completely subordinate to total human welfare.

It sounds fantastic. Can you imagine a day when wages and profits, dividends and money markets shall not be the prime concern of men and nations, when society is not divided up into classes by monetary standards? It sounds impossible, yet to the historian of some future century, when he turns over the pages of the past and reads the story of our times, what may strike him most is their barbarism. We cannot conceive such a verdict being passed upon our modern, scientific, enlightened age. But it will amaze him that an age presented with such amazing opportunities and possessed of the wealth, the skill, and the knowledge to develop them, yet preferred doles and distressed areas, blitzed cities and bloody wars rather than surrender its belief in the supremacy of money. Why did those moderns think that the multiplication of forms of cheap amusement, the building of greater and greater power machinery, the invention of aeroplanes and radio, represented progress, while all the time misery and malnutrition in their distressed areas, the drab godlessness of their great industrial cities, the merciless mechanical massacre of their wars, stood before their eyes to show them whither they were "progressing"? That to him will be the insoluble enigma.

Nor is such a mighty step forward in the life of man an economic impossibility. It would have been in the past when man's economics dealt with the problem of scarcity: but the amazing increase in productivity brought about by the perfecting of the machine, and the very fact that the trouble of modern times arises from over-production, shows that it is within the reach of practical politics. The financial cost of this war has reached figures which are nothing less than astronomical, but there is not the slightest danger that we shall lose the war through lack of money. Why? Because the object in view is worth the cost and sacrifice involved. It would take but a portion of that cost to abolish insecurity and want from our national life after the war; and if that morally right and practically feasible objective is not attained it will not be because economic factors forbid it. Then why can it not be done? Only because people cannot believe a social order possible in which it is taken for granted that every man who is prepared to work shall enjoy a reasonable standard of living. They are so inured to a world dominated by profits and prices, magnates and money markets, that they cannot imagine another. A "new world after the war" lies within their reach, a really new world, not a mere mitigation of the old, but they lack the faith and moral determination to take possession of it.

This war is the greatest disaster and the grandest opportunity that has occurred to man for centuries. "The unemployment problem," writes Professor Carr, "can be solved in time of war because war provides an aim deemed worthy of self-sacrifice. It cannot be solved in time of peace only because modern civilisation recognises no peace-time aim for which people are prepared to sacrifice themselves in the same way." What an indictment! Between the world of economic man and the world of human man there is a gulf fixed which needs a bridge to span it if future generations are to pass over. The materials required for the building of that bridge are faith, fellowship, and moral determination—and our clever world walks away and says, "Can't be done." The whole idea of a form of civilisation in which the economic motive is transcended, is put into its proper and subordinate place as man's servant instead of his master, is regarded as fantastic. But is it? Then why at this very hour does the fate of our country and the safety of our own lives depend upon men who have transcended the economic motive? It was not that motive which inspired our airmen in the battle of Britain. It is not that motive which at this moment is keeping our men fighting with dogged determination from Acroma to Bir Hakeim, in spite of the blazing heat, the clouds of dust, and the death-spitting tanks of Rommel's Panzer divisions. If the soldier and sailor only fought according to his pay he would be entitled to do mighty little fighting. As an economic proposition it is a very poor one.

The fact which stands out stark and undeniable before our eyes to-day is that our danger in this war lies in those who stay at home and scheme for the highest profits or fight for the highest wages, while our safety lies in those who move in a sphere where human values are the only ones that count, where bravery, sacrifice, loyalty to your pal, fellowship in the face of death, are the only form of wealth that matters. War has at least this merit that it reveals Truth. It strips off the lying mask which covers the face of peace-time living, and lays bare the patent fact (though men discard it as a platitude) that man's real wealth lies not in what he has, but in what he is. Our men saw that in the last war, and saw that a new world could be built upon it; that is why they hoped for "a land fit for heroes to live in". But they had forgotten that at home there were politicians, and magnates, and men of the world who were realists, men who knew that though the money game takes a back seat in wartime, it always presides when things return to normal.

"We lived many lives in those whirling campaigns," wrote Lawrence of Arabia, "yet when we achieved and the new world dawned, the old men came out again and took our victory to re-make it in the likeness of the former world they knew. . . . We stammered that we had worked for a new heaven and a new earth, and they thanked us kindly and made their peace." How true! And how damnable! So we buried the Unknown Warrior and set to work to build the land fit for the unemployed to lounge in. The only person who seems thoroughly determined that the human world shall replace the economic is God—so now we are at it again. They say God is a pacifist. Perhaps He is. But in nine wars out of ten He seems to be the only winner.

It will be a great step forward when the ordinary man realises that there is a moral structure to this universe as fixed and as inescapable as the laws which govern its physical frame. God is Perfect Love, but He is also Inexorable Will. Nothing is easier than to ignore both Him and His will, nothing more impossible than to escape the consequences of so doing. Under the pressure of that inexorable will the People's world will one day arise. But when? Will we begin to lay the foundations of it as soon as this war is over? Spengler says no. He bids us distrust those human-istic hopes and yearnings which man entertains when his civilisa-tion is on the decline. "In spite of its foreground appearances, ethical socialism is not a system of compassion, humanity, peace and kindly care, but one of will to power. . . . Amongst us senti-mental morale, morale directed to happiness and usefulness is

never the final instinct, however we may persuade ourselves
otherwise."[1] On the contrary, socialism of necessity leads, he says,
to Caesarism, because the "dictature of money" can only be
broken by force. In his cyclical theory of history (i.e. the theory
that every civilisation follows the life course of man himself, birth,
growth, decay, death) it is Caesarism, and the atheism which
accompanies it, which betoken the approaching end—and there
is no escaping it. "For us whom a Destiny has placed in this
culture and at this moment of its development—the moment
when money is celebrating its last victories, and the Caesarism
that is to succeed approaches with quiet, firm step—our direction,
willed and obligatory at once, is set for us within narrow limits,
and on any other terms life is not worth the living. We have not
the freedom to reach to this or to that, but the freedom to do the
necessary or do nothing."

One would pay no attention to a reading of history so fatalistic
and pessimistic were it not that the wealth of evidence which he
brings to bear from all the civilisations of the past seems to prove
conclusively the truth of his "cyclical" theory. It may be true
of history as it has been. No civilisation yet has escaped the
temptation to seek greatness in Imperialism and financial wealth.
The lust to conquer and to possess has always seized it sooner or
later, and it is this materialism which has dug the grave of every
empire that has flourished and fallen. And since living matter
can only follow nature's course of birth, growth, decay, and death,
how can any empire or civilisation, rooted in the principles of
matter, i.e. in Materialism, avoid the same fate? What Spengler
does not allow for is this, that if a civilisation were founded on a
moral concept instead of on a materialistic creed, it would *ipso
facto* escape that deadly cycle of inescapable destiny. Love, truth,
justice, beauty, goodness—these do not belong to the time order
and are not subject to its cyclical course. Why then should a
civilisation which put culture before cash, God before gold,
man before money, the moral motive of world-building before
the material motive of world-conquest, suffer this melancholy
fate?

Is not that just the choice that lies before man to-day at this
fateful moment in his history? "Speak to the children of Israel
that they go forward"—such is the command of God that comes
to us above the noise and din of battle. It means an enormous
and unprecedented step forward in the moral, social, and political
life of man; yet if it is not taken Spengler may well prove correct.
"The changing theme of history," "transcending the economic
motive"—we see now what they mean; they represent a line of

[1] Spengler, *The Decline of the West.*

action clear, consistent, and practical, but requiring an enormous
moral dynamic to carry it through.

Can the Church provide it? If it fails to do so its interest in
social reform will prove of no account. So we have come back
to our original conclusion that the problem lies primarily in the
man, not in the plan. It is a dangerous fallacy to think that the
correct diagnosis of a situation is sufficient for its cure. All that
the intellect can do is to investigate and analyse the factors and
forces underlying the world situation of to-day, and prescribe the
measures necessary for a more just, equal and stable order of
society. It cannot generate the motive power necessary to ensure
the carrying out of those measures. Blue-prints may provide
light, they do not generate heat. It was not the dialectical
materialism of Karl Marx which stirred the Russian masses and
made communism spread like a prairie fire through the land.
It was the slogan, "Workers of the world unite!" And in that
call is hidden a powerful moral appeal to something which lies
deep in the human heart, namely, a yearning for the day when
"man to man the wide world o'er shall brothers be for a' that".
It is natural perhaps for a sophisticated and highly intellectual
age to scorn the suggestion that the remedy for its troubles is
biological and elementary, rather than technical and complex.
It has achieved such mastery over the forces of nature by its
scientific discoveries, that is to say, by the power of the brain,
that it is sure the conquest of the future too will come about in
the same way. So it sets itself to discover the brilliant politico-
economic scheme which will unlock the doors to the future. It is
so obsessed with the desire to "understand all mysteries and all
knowledge" that it is completely blind to the fact that without
love that knowledge "profiteth nothing". Not even with this war
before its eyes, a war which is the most terrible demonstration
of the truth of St. Paul's assertion, can it be brought to see its
mistake. Yet evidence abounds on every hand—in the apathy
towards Parliamentary politics, in the indifference towards
religion, in the boredom and futility of living of which people
are acutely conscious and from which they wish to God they could
escape. This is not a malady which the brain can cure because
it is a failure in living, and only new life can overcome it.

"It is the Spirit which giveth life." To mediate and purvey
that Spirit to the life of man is the supreme function and prime
duty of the Church. If it fails in that duty no amount of conferences and manifestos concerned with the Christian Social
Order will make good the failure. As Miss Evelyn Underhill says,
"If the swing over to a purely social interpretation of religion be
allowed to continue unchecked, the result can only be an

impoverishment of our spiritual life quite as far-reaching and regrettable as that which follows from an unbridled individual-ism." Nor is it sufficient to reply that through the Church's sacramental ministry that Spirit is continually mediated to man. It is. And yet it is hard to believe that our Anglican Communion is an effective spirit-filled body. Theoretically, yes; but the people do not find it so. There is a dull, uninspiring mediocrity in its institutional life which is not only the target of criticism for the laity, but a source of anxiety to earnest priests themselves. Many clergy are as acutely conscious of frustration in their ministerial calling as the people are in their daily lives. "What are we getting at?", "When is something going to happen?", "When is somebody going to give us a lead?"—those are the questions which clergy are asking themselves in their study, and which the laity are asking themselves in the street.

I know it can and will be answered that there have been times in the past when the Church has been far more dead than it is to-day. But there also have been times in the past when it experienced a renewing of its energies and a revitalising of its life which made it a power and a blessing to the people of that age. *Nothing less than that will meet the needs of our land to-day.* Let us face that fact squarely, and give up excusing, defending, and justifying the state of things as they are. If there are politicians who will not see that they are completely out of touch with the feelings and wishes of the people, so are there ecclesiastics who are fatuously and wilfully blind to what people think about the Church. It never occurs to them that the present apathy towards the Church may turn to irritation, and from irritation to hostility. Nor if that day of hostility came, would they be other than completely dumbfounded as to the reason for it, and quite sure that no blame for it could be attributed to the Church itself.

It is the danger of every institution that in the course of time it tends to destroy the inspiration it was designed to conserve. The forms remain, but from them the life has flown. Is it not possible that that is the basic source of the heaviness and dryness which beset the Church to-day? If it is, no amount of interest in social reform will avail to restore its life. Such activities will tend to re-arouse interest in the Church, they will make the outside world realise that the Church is awake to the needs of the day and is doing its best to play its part in the struggle for a new and better world. But if there is a drying-up of the springs which water its own life from within, any re-animation which such activities may beget will be purely temporary.

It is most necessary that in every age the Gospel should be preached in the terms of that age and related as closely as possible to its needs, conditions, and problems. But it is necessary also that the Church in trying to do that should not allow itself to be carried away by the popular current. During the past fifty years there has been an enormous amount of research into the origin and historical value of the books of the Bible, and much scholarship of a high order applied to restating and re-shaping theological doctrines, as required by new knowledge and new modes of thought. The gain which has resulted is unquestioned. But we were living in a scientific age, and that was the scientific spirit applied to the sphere of religion. We thought we were leading; actually we were following. It was necessary to do so, but we should have borne in mind our danger, the danger of thinking that the Church could be revitalised by intellectual means. It was hoped that when we had removed the religious difficulties modern man found in the way of believing, he would come back to the Church. But did he? God is not found at the end of argument, nor is He something to be conquered as science by its intellectual power has conquered the secrets of the earth.

So we should be careful to-day. Socialism is in fashion, and social and economic problems are the problems of the hour. It were folly to ignore that fact, but greater folly to forget that our prime duty is to proclaim the eternal, to hold up before man the Eternal Truth, clean and bright above the changing clouds of temporal affairs. Christianity is a this-worldly religion, it is meant to be applied to the actual needs of the here and now. But its very essence and its essential power come from its otherworldliness. Once the Church loosens its hold on that vital truth it will become stranded in the shallow waters of contemporary affairs. There is additional point and special urgency at the moment in the prayer of the Church that "we may so pass through things temporal that we lose not the things eternal". Clerical conferences convened to discuss the application of Christian principles to the working life of the nation usually succeed in generating interest in the subject and in throwing light on some of the intricacies and difficulties involved in the undertaking. But all too often the atmosphere pervading such meetings is too near to that of political controversy and secular debate. We must come down to the concrete and particular, but we ought to come down to them "from the Mount". Such a warning may sound trite and conventional, but nothing can alter the fact that Our Lord carried about with Him the atmosphere of the Eternal, and it was that atmosphere which made the deepest impression on His hearers. His work can only be done in this way. Holiness is not only that without which no man shall see the Lord, it is also that without which no man can do His work.

No one will question the part which the later Tractarians played in fighting against the social evils of capitalism as seen in all their foulness in the slums of our great cities where so many of them worked. Nor should we forget the debt we owe to them for reminding the Church that her gospel has a vital social content. But when one reads the life of a Lowder or a Dolling how different is the spirit which permeated their labours from that which pervades social reform activities to-day! They were aflame for social righteousness, but the flame was one which was taken from the altar and tended in the silence of daily meditation. They were splendidly this-worldly in the courage of their fighting, but grandly other-worldly in the source of their power. Hence in their lives we catch the authentic note of Him who "had compassion on the multitudes". It is the absence of that note which gives to much of the Christian sociology of to-day a technical rather than a spiritual flavour. It is man-centred rather than God-centred. The vision of God's rule on earth to which the early Christian looked forward in faith, and for which he gave himself to a life of prayer, discipline, and ceaseless loving service seems to have faded. The best our modern world seems able to envisage is a socialist Utopia with a vague religious background. I can conceive of few things more fatal to the religious life of man than a secular Utopia. Having food and clothing the people will therewith be content to leave religion alone! "Why worry?"

Nothing can alter the fact that the prime duty of the Church is to produce that holiness, that otherness, which alone can rescue the world from its deadly materialism and secularism. That the communist will denounce it as "pie in the sky", that the average man will say he is only interested in practical religion, must not deter us. Any short cut to the Kingdom of God, which by-passes the tasking road of holiness, will in the end prove disastrous.

Can we hope to see in the near future a movement arising within the Church, which will bear its own distinctive witness and make its own distinctive contribution to the building of that better and happier world of the future which man so sorely needs and God so surely wills? It must be a movement which does not confine itself merely to the enunciation of general principles, but which does its utmost to encourage and support any party or any person propounding particular measures which will effect a change-over to a Christian basis of society; but which nevertheless refuses to lose its identity in humanitarian socialism and insists that the new order "cometh down from Heaven", maintains, above all things, the supremacy of God, and asserts that salvation lies in incarnating His will rather than in implementing human wishes.

The fact that the Church is now awake to the need of "putting its house in order" would seem to encourage that hope. There are stirrings to-day within the Church which may betoken the revival of its life and the renewal of its power. But history offers few examples of an institution which effects its own revival. In the majority of cases that is brought about by a Minority Movement within its borders. Christianity was itself such a movement, so was Franciscanism, so was Wesleyanism, so was Tractarianism. It is in that direction we should look to-day, and look with faith and expectation. So far we have got no further than experimental "groups", but it is my belief that eventually there will arise from them a Leader and a Minority Movement which will restore to the Church that "newness of life" for which we thirst. It will also, I hope, be accompanied by the vision of that "oecumenical Christianity", that vision of the Church as a world-wide fellowship which holds more hope for the restoration of Christendom and for the future happiness of mankind than any earthly reforms can ever effect.

But space forbids me to speak of these matters in detail: I have only ventured to suggest that if in the turmoil of to-day a new world is struggling to be born, it will need in the Church wider vision, greater daring, and a more utter faithfulness to God, if it is to help that world to birth.

I believe that renewal of its life will come; but if it does not, then when like Peter of old we ask Him, "*Domine, quo vadis?*", He will look us sadly in the face, and say, "I go to Rome to be crucified instead of thee".

Malvern declared: "*Every child should find itself a member of a family housed with decency and dignity. Every adult, fulfilling his or her lawful function as citizen and worker, should be secure in possession of such income as will enable him to maintain a home and to bring up children. Every citizen should have sufficient leisure to enable him to enjoy a full personal and family life.*" The family is the basis of Christian civilisation. Family life is robbed of "*decency and dignity*" by social conditions—by foul housing, by malnutrition, by economic insecurity—and, because of his concern for the home, the Christian must be concerned with the crusade against these evils.

It is obvious that no satisfactory family life is possible unless the physical well-being of parents and children is safeguarded. Health depends on adequate food and decent housing. In his latest book, Fighting for What?, Sir John Orr says: "*The standard of living of a third of the population is below the level needed for health either in food or housing and, in the case of the poorest, in both. . . . It is not sufficiently realised that, in some towns and cities, there are thousands of families living in houses unfit for human habitation, and families which have not even the elementary sanitary convenience of a W.C. of their own. Among the families of the unemployed and of the poorest paid workers, more than one infant in ten dies soon after it is born because the mothers are badly fed and badly housed.*"

It was fully realised at Malvern that since Christians realise the supreme importance of a decent and dignified family life they must be concerned with the social and economic changes that are necessary to ensure the conditions that make such a life possible for, not a fortunate minority, but for all. More even than sufficient food and a sanitary and convenient house is needed if the family is to fulfill its divinely intended function. Spiritual health is destroyed by the fear that darkens the homes of the poor that the scanty wages this week may be non-existent next week, and that the wage earner will become, against his will, an idler, with his manhood sapped by daily disappointments at the Labour Exchanges and his children dependent on the dole. Unemployment degrades the man and breaks the spirit of his wife.

It is, therefore, idle to hold up high ideals of family life so long as insecurity, malnutrition and foul housing continue, and it is concern for these ideals that inspires the demand for what Dr. Temple has called a Christian revolution.

The Christian declares that work with adequate wages shall be secured for all, that for every family there shall be a good home, that there shall be common facilities for the enjoyment of leisure, that there shall be such training and encouragement for all as will help towards the appreciation of art and literature and of the beauty of God's fair world, because of his conviction that all these things are vital for the happy family life, sanctified by our Lord when He lived with His Mother and St. Joseph in Nazareth.

But the Christian also knows (this was emphasised at Malvern) that social changes will not of themselves secure the Christian home. In the following essay the Bishop of Chelmsford, who is himself among the most earnest social reformers, insists that there must be the consecration of the individual, or the well-filled larder and all the modern contraptions of the house will have no spiritual value. The beginning of the Christian home is the Christian marriage which the Bishop says is "human friendship at its highest level consecrated by the benediction of God".

The primary responsibility for the material and spiritual well-being of children is the parents'. But the community has its responsibility too. "To rear a family is to enrich society," and society has an obvious duty to ensure the conditions without which parental responsibility cannot be adequately fulfilled.

THE FAMILY AND THE HOME

By The Bishop of Chelmsford

THERE is nothing so characteristic of our national and social life as the home. We are not at all inclined to become sentimental over it, chiefly because we regard it as an established institution which can be taken for granted as an integral part of the national habit and inheritance: nevertheless there is a real and sincere reverence for it as something vital to personal happiness and social well-being. The criticism of "advanced thinkers" is borne with patience; and usually some measure of agreement is given to the disparagement of the Victorian homes, the iron discipline of the father, the magnitude of the family, the subjection of the children, the need for thrifty living and so on, though it would be a bold or ignorant person who would deny that the product of those homes was usually strong, adventurous, healthy in character and forceful in personality.

The general reaction to all this is good-tempered indifference, for it is taken for granted that all that we mean by home is such a permanent element in our life and so built into the foundations of our traditions and way of life that criticism and even disparagement will do no harm.

But all this is very dangerous. No sensible person would maintain that much of the criticism of the home of even fifty years ago is without justification, but it is little realised that it is not a type of home-life which is called in question to-day so much as the very institution itself; a whole set of circumstances of the most varied character are challenging the rightfulness as well as the possibilities of the continued existence of home. To use a lurid illustrative phrase, half a dozen "pincer movements" are steadily and relentlessly at work to "pinch out" the home altogether.

The frequency of divorce is so alarming that in almost any drawing-room full of people great care must be exercised lest an awkward situation is created by a tactless remark; and yet divorce is so lightly regarded that it would probably only be the speaker who would feel awkward! Again, families are becoming more and more scarce and smaller and smaller in size. One child or at most two is the usual product of a marriage. The economic problem, or the desire to be unrestrained in the enjoyment of life, is reducing the population in a most alarming fashion. The shortage of domestic help is resulting in widespread abandonment of house-keeping. The well-to-do often live in hotels or boarding

houses with their progeny of one or two precocious children, who
in consequence will never know what happy childhood means:
the less prosperous commonly eat at national restaurants and
communal feeding centres, and the family meal is becoming
almost an unusual experience. The evacuation of homes in
consequence of the war, the absence of the father on war service,
and of the mother, engaged in some form of national work, have
resulted in the scattering of the family and the disintegration of
home-life. To all these social complications which are under-
mining the foundations of our social life must be added yet
another and more dangerous enemy. There is current a new
theory of morality which is, in practice, an attempt to justify on
supposed psychological grounds what would have been called
fifty years ago "sexual debauchery". This theory proclaims that
every person should have complete sexual freedom; husbands and
wives should not object to, not even be jealous of, one another's
"romantic" adventures and to pretend that a marriage pledge
should be considered as any restraint upon conduct is both unreasonable and unscientific. Such teaching lays down that
paternal feeling is a relic which higher civilization is steadily
weakening: the creation of a family is a rather out-moded per-
formance, not altogether to be roundly condemned provided the
children are not repressed and over-disciplined, but nevertheless
an institution which will probably pass out altogether when the
State takes over the responsibility for maintaining the population
and the upbringing of the children of the nation in public nurseries.

Extravagant though all this may sound it has poisoned the air
in a terrible fashion. To adhere to a strict moral code is to be
out of date, to regard loose morals as in any way wrong is not
only stupid and unreasonable but unscientific. To demand high
moral standards is to accept the obsolete conventions of the age
of crinolines, antimacassars and Dundreary whiskers. Man has
learnt better now. His new code of conduct is more free and he
can, and indeed should "let himself go", for the great good is the
unrestrained expression of himself (or herself) particularly since
any attempt to curb nature will probably result in complexes or
repressions which might have the most lamentable results. Sir
Galahad is now dubbed a fool and Don Juan has become the
example for all modern people of intelligence to emulate; Messa-
lina is an excellent model for all girls and matrons.[1] Vice has
become sensible and morality is simple stupidity.

[1] In *The Times* newspaper, May 26th, 1942, there is a report on the Registrar-
General's review of the population in 1938, which is not yet published owing to the
paper shortage. This reveals that "about 40 per cent of women married before
20 years of age must have been pregnant before marriage: the proportion was about
30 per cent for those who married at 20 and about 20 per cent for those who married
at 21."

Such in brief summary is the situation which is steadily, and in some directions rapidly, unfolding itself and it is clear that the general assumption that the home is a solid factor in our social life has ever-diminishing justification. There is a rot in the foundations.

There is need, therefore, for a defence of the home: some positive statement of its claims and its possibilities, for it cannot be taken for granted that it will stand unshaken in face of the attack being made upon it from so many different quarters. Moreover, it is, as we know it, a Christian institution and the basis of Christian social life. It was always tacitly assumed that both the home and the underlying moral principles upon which it was based were securely entrenched behind the impregnable defence of the Christian Faith. But now the Christian Religion is itself assailed, called in question, denied or ignored as an obsolete thing in modern life. This, in brief, is the situation which confronts us to-day.

The home is society in a microcosm. It is the result of an evolutionary process which has been carefully traced by sociologists but, as we know it, it has taken its definite shape largely upon the ideal held by the Jews, though some of the features they stamped on it have been either modified or have disappeared altogether. But the peculiar sanctity impressed upon it by the Jews has for the Christian received a higher significance still because the Incarnate Son of God was Himself a member of a home and from that time onwards motherhood, fatherhood, the relation of children to parents and to one another, have been refined, elevated and sanctified and the Christian home has been recognised as the highest and holiest environment in which parents and children can dwell together, and the happiest condition in which a human being can live. Such is still the claim of the Christian.

The home is the institution which presents humanity with the fullest opportunity for happiness and that of the most varied kind. It has been said that the greatest earthly success is to achieve happiness at home, and few popular sayings are so obviously true, but a happy home can only be built upon solid foundations, for it is such a highly complex and delicate institution and round it are gathered so many problems, political, social, moral and economic, any one of which can almost wreck the whole structure, that it cannot be said too emphatically that a durable foundation is a vital necessity.

The home offers scope to all the best qualities possessed by man: and also to the worst! Unselfishness, loyal friendship, self-discipline,

2

devotion to hard work for the sake of others, sympathy, delicate understanding of human nature, all of these and many more, are called for therein. In the home man can attain to his highest or fall to his lowest: at home he can be his best or his worst. The prize of a happy home is great and is worth every effort in the winning, but it will call not only for constant striving but for the grace of God. The Christian Church has never been in any doubt on this point. It has never pretended that the strain and responsibility, perhaps the monotony and even the penury that have to be endured, are unreal or can be easily borne. But it does claim that there is joy in service and sacrifice, and that the Grace of God can enable man to rejoice in these things and in the little world of his home, to be perfectly happy and to live in an atmosphere of love and peace, and having those things he may enjoy the best that life can give.

A right understanding of marriage is essential for the creation of a happy home. This is all the more needful because the consideration of marriage can easily be confused by a wrong perspective, which silhouettes it against the murky horizon of the sex problems which have opened out such a wide field of activity for cranks, oddities and moral eccentrics. The advocates of companionate marriage, free sexual expression, "marriage" terminable if the experiment is unsuccessful, have had such a long run that not only is the Christian ideal often regarded as a lost cause, but its defender is looked upon as a pitiful obscurantist who fails to recognise that sex problems have always been the main preoccupation of everybody and particularly so to-day.

The consideration of marriage is not helped greatly either by the Preface to the Marriage Service in the Book of Common Prayer or even by the revised form of that Preface in the amended book of 1928. In the latter the wording is made less direct and relieved of some of its crudities but the order of the purposes for which marriage was ordained is wrong in both versions. The primary purpose of marriage, which is placed *third* on the list in both prayer books, is, according to the ancient tradition, "the mutual society, help, and comfort which the one ought to have of the other", and it is singularly unfortunate and misleading that this is made subordinate to the creation of the family and the hallowing of sex.

A profound understanding of the human heart is disclosed in the old record:

"And the Lord God said: It is not good, that the man should be alone, I will make him an help meet for him."

We shall never see marriage in its true light, much less realise its happiness, until we grasp the fact that the duty of parentage and the satisfaction of the sexual instinct are both secondary to the view of marriage as primarily sanctified friendship. It is at that point that the start must be made in the quest for a happy married life.

Man lives in the herd. He is one of the crowd and the supreme torture is isolation from his kind. But in his inmost self he desires something more, something deeper, than the casual association with the many and the more close friendship with the few. He wants one friend with whom he stands unchallengeably first, one friend upon whom he can utterly depend, who will love him to the end, whatever he becomes, whether he sinks to obscurity or rises to the heights of success: someone who will love him with utter loyalty and stand at his side even if he is disgraced, shamed and forsaken by the whole world, someone who will die in the ditch with him rather than forsake him. He wants his wife.

Similarly with the woman. She wants her husband: no shining knight of heroic splendour and gallant form, but one upon whose loyalty to her she cannot merely rely but which is of such a kind that it will never cross her mind to question its reliability. He may be a very unromantic figure, whom age has robbed of all physical attraction, whose habits and mannerisms are commonplace and even exasperating. But she wants to know that there is someone in the world's wilderness whose unfaltering friendship she can take as an assured fact and so enable her to build her life upon the foundation of a love which will never forsake her.

I believe that this is not merely the best and the most helpful approach to an understanding of marriage, but that it is the true approach and by taking it half the problems commonly associated with marriage disappear and the other half are easily solved.

The general argument, for instance, upon which the pleadings for the Herbert Act were based was the hardship endured by the desertion, the lifelong imprisonment or the "incurable" insanity of one's partner. The answer to the Christian to all this is: here is the very opportunity for lifelong loyalty to show its mettle. The criminal shall at least know that his wife has not forsaken him. The poor sufferer in the mental home may have the light of reason return if only in fitful glimmers, but she shall then know that the faithful heart is faithful still. The deserter may return and if he does he will see the light in the window. The feeble arguments based upon hardship and the destruction of personal happiness are seen to belong to a mean and shabby world of sordid and selfish values.

Marriage, as the Christian sees it, is human friendship at its highest level consecrated by the benediction of God, and every other aspect of the contract is secondary to that. It is human love in its supreme form, and it is the failure to grasp this fact which is the root of all matrimonial perplexities and disaster. For immediately the argument is admitted that the contract is breakable if it causes extreme hardship upon one or both of the partners, then the vision vanishes and we are left with an institution which is little more than legalised concubinage terminable at will. This may sound a hard judgment to pass upon recent legislation, but it is inevitable. For once the argument from hardship is admitted it becomes impossible to define precisely what degree of hardship is required by law to dissolve the contract. Is the husband whose wife is a shrew suffering less hardship than he whose wife is in a mental home? Certainly not! Is the wife whose husband lives at his club and returns home regularly in a fuddled state happier than she whose husband has definitely deserted her? That is very doubtful. Reno is at least logical in its legislation, and it is as certain as that the sun is in the skies that our divorce laws will in course of time deteriorate in the same direction.[1]

But the view of marriage as sanctified friendship has been prejudiced by a sex-obsession which has disclosed itself in two entirely contrary theories: one a recoil from the sex-instinct and the other an insistence that the sex-instinct exercises a complete mastery over the thinking self.

The former of these theories was prevalent in the early years of the Roman Empire and is not without its adherents to-day. In its extreme form it taught that sex was an unholy thing and something which must be banished by all who desired to live their lives on the highest level. It was grudgingly conceded that the matron's life was not positively displeasing to God, but it was definitely on a lower level than that of a virgin. Though this view is now obsolete the suspicion that sex is really a rather nasty business, which no one should talk about except with a blush and in lowered tones, is in fact due to the same cause as the ascetic abhorrence of marriage.

At the other extreme is the theory which now finds expression in an impressive psychological theory that sex is the dominant factor in human life. All actions and reactions are traceable to it: the sex urge and sex-expression control behaviour in all men and women. There is little in this theory which could claim to

[1] An illustration is afforded in the *Sunday Dispatch*, April 20th, 1942. when Professor C. E. M. Joad, in answer to a correspondent, replied as follows: "Inevitably one's sentiments change. I believe it would lead to a real increase in happiness if we made provision for that change of sentiment in our institutions, which means making marriage dissoluble at the will of either partner, provided that that will is persistently maintained over a reasonable period, say twelve months." This is of course perfectly reasonable if the lower view of marriage is held. But why twelve months? Why not twelve days or hours or minutes!! Why marry at all?

be based on sound scientific processes; it is at the best, a hypothesis supported by ingenious special pleading, and at worst it lends itself to a pretended scientific justification of indiscriminate sexual indulgence, described as the free expression of the emotions, which it is claimed is the right of all properly functioning persons.

That there are people, both men and women, of this unbalanced type, which this psychological theory declares to be the common state of all, no one would deny. But there are people who are unbalanced in other ways, gluttons, drunkards, misers; and by the same process of special pleading it would be easy for an ingenious person to build up an equally impressive theory that all men and women are dominated by the passion to eat or drink to excess, or that the supreme and universal human instinct is greed. Cranks can indeed prove almost anything they please provided they have definitely made up their mind as to the conclusion they intend to arrive at and can display sufficient ingenuity in manipulating or manufacturing evidence.

Marriage as the Christian conceives it is an institution designed by God for man's highest happiness and from the human point of view based upon the highest human instincts, man's capacity for self-sacrificing love and disregard of his own comfort in the quest of a great achievement, and not on the lower instincts which can so easily degenerate, if allowed to obtain the mastery, into mere animalism.

No one supposes that it is easy to realise the ideal. The grace of God is indispensable to success: the grace of God which supplies the love which "suffereth long and is kind, envieth not, vaunteth not itself, seeketh not its own, is not provoked, thinketh no evil, beareth all things, believeth all things, hopeth all things, endureth all things." Bluntly stated, here is something which is not easily attained for it is definitely a divine gift, and the kind of language which the Christian uses to describe marriage as he sees it bears little resemblance to that used by those whose approach to it begins with emphasis upon the sexual aspects. If it is thought of as a means of getting for one's own sake rather than as an opportunity of giving for the sake of someone else, the result will never be other than disappointment and frequently disaster. God must be brought into the contract if self-sacrificing love, without which happy marriage is impossible, is to be obtained. Dr. Samuel Johnson put the matter well when he declared that Christian marriage was not a contract between two, a man and a woman, but between three, a man, a woman and God.

The tragedy is that the whole picture has been distorted by the fatal postulate that personal happiness is the supreme end in life and the corollary that happiness cannot be obtained without sexual satisfaction. This results in the futile attempt to build up a theory of marriage upon a foundation of sand. The passions then become such a dominant feature in the landscape that there is no room for the affections: love is crowded out by lust. Marriage becomes not a sacred contract but a convenient way of living which can be and should be abandoned wherever it ceases to minister to the happiness of the contracting parties. This is in reality the logic underlying the demand for the extension of the grounds for divorce.

The Christian view of marriage can be conveniently summarised as follows: A man and woman pledge themselves, under the benediction of God, to lifelong fellowship with one another because they cannot contemplate life without the constant companionship of each other. That companionship finds its inevitable expression in the supreme act of love between man and woman and that act of love issues normally in the creation of children who, because they are the product, under God, of the bodies of the father and mother become additional bonds to unite in closer love the lives of the parents.

It is not practically possible to discuss the whole range of questions and problems associated with marriage but it must be positively stated that the wholehearted acceptance of the Christian standard goes a very long way towards their answer and solution, apart from the fact that, for the Christian, many of them don't arise at all.

It is commonly said that ignorance about matters of sex is responsible for much immorality among young people and is often the seed of unhappiness in marriage. It may be doubted whether there is much ignorance on these subjects to-day but, generally speaking, it is probable that the instruction is given in the wrong way and by the wrong people.

The right people are the parents and their duty in this direction should not be regarded as a difficult business calling for expert handling. Surely the obvious thing to do is for the parents to regard reference to sex questions as part of those elementary matters relating to personal hygiene which every sensible parent would explain to children! The normal functions of the body should always be made clear to the child and knowledge of the sexual organs and the importance of their care is no more delicate a business (particularly if the child has not yet become sexually self-conscious) than a warning of the danger of constipation and emphasis upon the importance of keeping the teeth clean. Nothing is more calculated to awaken unhealthy thoughts in a boy or girl than the impression that some dark secret shrouds one particular part of the body and on the other hand the sure prevention of unhealthy thinking is to make the child acquainted, in early years, when no prurient interest attaches to the subject, with the general functioning of the sex organs.

An equally great need is the instruction of young people who are about to marry in the meaning and ideals of Christian Marriage; for marriage, as the Christian understands it, is something very different from the light-hearted affair, which is frequently regarded with flippancy and even coarseness. It is worth every effort to impress a high ideal upon an engaged couple at a time when they are peculiarly impressionable. If the Christian Church is to reinstate marriage this must be regarded as the rule and not the exception, for there are so many forces at work tending to lower the character of marriage that the Church should take a definite stand at this point. Two or three interviews with the clergyman who is going to take the marriage service should be required before the ceremony. In one exceptionally large parish, where many marriages take place, special services for people about to get married are held and the young couples eagerly attend to hear friendly talks and fatherly advice upon the beautiful thing which they are about to do and the splendid prospect of living a married life blessed by God. This is the best corrective for the vulgar and debased views on marriage which are current to-day.

The use of contraceptive devices has raised a great problem upon which a few words must be said. Here is a new situation which the Christian Church must squarely face. There is a dishonest evasion of the issue which is tempting enough: to set up an official standard which in practice no one is expected to observe. Or the Church might not only prohibit the practice but put under severe discipline those who defied the prohibition— assuming that the offenders could be detected! Neither of these policies can be regarded as a satisfactory treatment of the matter. The following illustration may help in indicating a right line of approach. A problem of a very different kind presented itself in the early church but the apostolic ruling then given indicates principles which we might well bear in mind in facing our difficulty.

The Christians, of course, mixed intimately with the pagans in business and social affairs, and it frequently happened that when enjoying the hospitality of a pagan friend, the meat set before the Christian was that which had been offered in sacrifice to the heathen gods. What was the Christian to do in such cases? There were some who said that to eat such meat was to participate in heathen worship, and the over-scrupulous went so far as to advocate complete vegetarianism lest by some accident such meat might be eaten. There were others who argued that idols were nothing, heathen gods were non-existent, and that, therefore, the strong line to take was to show disregard for heathen ideas and eat without scruple.

St. Paul's ruling was that if a man's conscience were untroubled when he ate, then for him eating was no sin. But while thus recognising the sovereign right of conscience, he made clear that a man owed a duty, in the exercise of his conscientious liberty, to the brethren of more sensitive type, and that the law of love should restrain him from so using his liberty as to become a stumbling-block to others. The parallel is obviously not exact but it does lay down general principles of wide application. It is not always possible to describe particular acts as sinful or virtuous. These are borderline cases and in such cases conscience has its rights but love should always be in control.

The facts which must be faced include the following:

1. The sexual act, in the words of the Lambeth Conference, 1930, resolution, "has a value of its own within that sacrament and thereby married love is enhanced and its character strengthened." In other words intercourse can be an end in itself as fostering love and should not be regarded as restricted only to those times when the birth of a child is desired.

2. The spacing of the family, it is said, is desirable on social and economic grounds, and since long abstinence could not reasonably be expected, particularly in view of the value of the sexual act in strengthening love, some liberty must be allowed.

3. Many people, not merely the peculiarly scrupulous, feel intuitively that the practice is wrong and they are unable to associate it with love in the purest sense, which is spontaneous in its expression.

4. On the other hand there are people equally sincere who feel no such reaction against the practice.

5. There are people who are so highly-sexed that it is unreasonable to expect from them long periods of abstinence and the health of the wife of such a person might not permit her to give birth to a child too frequently.

6. A wife might have conscientious objections to the use of such devices and also feel indisposed to bear a large family. As a result the husband might go elsewhere and the home disintegrate.

In reply to all this (and a good deal more which might be advanced) only a few general remarks can be made.

It would clearly be unjustifiable for the Church to denounce as sin a practice which many honest people are conscientiously convinced is *not* sinful. The maintenance of the integrity of the home is the prime necessity, and there is grave danger in attempting to enforce standards of the most exacting kind upon people whose consciences do not regard the practice as sinful at all. It is very easy to create new sins and the history of the Puritans reveals the deplorable reactions which can take place. But at the same time the very fact that many wise people regard the practice with grave concern and that many, not so scrupulous, do regard it as, at best, not in accordance with the highest standard of love, should provoke Christian people to question themselves very seriously. Here is surely a subject upon which the advice of a wise counsellor should be asked. Few clergymen in real touch with their people will deny the complications of the problem and none, save those who have little understanding of the difficulties of others, will consider that mere denunciation achieves anything but harm.

No consideration of the home would be complete unless some attention was given to the problem which is created in the home wrecked by divorce; but here again the subject is so many-sided that complete treatment is not possible. Great though the problem is in magnitude it is rapidly becoming greater, for though the increase in the number of divorces has advanced from 577 in 1913 to 7,955 in 1939, the effect of the Herbert Act, which permits divorce for several other reasons than adultery, will be to add enormously to that total.

It is, of course, out of the question that the Christian Church should even consider accommodating its moral standard to this situation, all the more so in view of the additional grounds recently legalised for divorce, since whatever may be said in defence of divorce after adultery, and the remarriage of the persons concerned (a matter upon which the authority of Christ can be invoked, somewhat ambiguous though the words are), there is beyond all dispute no vestige of authority in the New Testament for divorce on any other grounds.

Nevertheless, here is a situation rapidly assuming such dimensions that a very considerable proportion of the population will be involved in it, in one way or another, and for the Church to regard that section as practically isolated from its ministrations is really unthinkable. The time is hardly ripe for the setting out of any comprehensive policy but there are two or three considerations of a fundamental kind which must be borne in mind if a satisfactory Christian solution is to be achieved.

One such consideration is the welfare of the children and the rebuilding, so far as possible, of the home. Public opinion, which is so much centred on the grievances suffered by an unhappy married couple, should be (and probably could be by the right propaganda) switched over to the grievances of the children whose home-like is being destroyed by parents who put their own happiness before that of their children. A good deal might be done to "stop the rot" if public opinion looked with disfavour upon parents who disregard the rights of their children in this way, and regarded their conduct as grossly unselfish and anti-social.

Another such consideration is surely that the saving of a soul is of greater importance than the maintenance of rigid discipline. "I will have mercy and not sacrifice" is the kind of slogan which should guide the Church's policy in such a matter. It is a very terrible thing to refuse Communion to *anyone* and the automatic operation of general excommunication upon all divorced people would be a policy indefensible, and incompatible with the Christian valuation of the human soul.

The recent discussion of this subject in the Houses of Convocation seemed, at least to some people, curiously misdirected. The basic assumption appeared to be that large numbers of divorced people were eager to come to the Holy Communion and the Church was to decide upon what terms this could be allowed. Whether or not that assumption is correct we need not inquire, for in fact the real situation is very different. The common reaction of divorced people is to assume that they are outcast and that they are beyond the pale, and the reaction of this upon themselves and their children is obviously deplorable and presents a problem which a faithful church cannot ignore. The rebuilding of the broken home, the re-creation of decent surroundings for the children, and the salvation of the souls who have drifted away, are all matters of supreme concern to the Church and of far greater importance than a rigid and inflexible discipline which erects insurmountable barriers to exclude from Divine Grace the people who need it most.

It is not easy to outline a policy but it is quite easy to lay down the principles which should guide its formulation. It must suffice here to say that each case should be dealt with on its own merits and that instead of a rather grudging consent to admit divorced people to the Communion, hedged round by all sorts of conditions, the Church should set out to seek for these people and by love and sympathy endeavour to help in the rebuilding of the home and the reclaiming of those who have fallen away.

In these days when life is so complicated by social and economic problems, the parents who enter upon the adventure of rearing a family are giving many hostages to fortune. About that there is no doubt; but it needs to be boldly stated that this pre-occupation with difficulties, obstacles, complications and anxieties has resulted in married people refusing to take the road which leads to the real happiness and solid joy which can be found only in the creation and training of a family. The Old Testament teaching was based upon the perfect understanding of human nature. There it is taught that the childless marriage is a calamity; "the quiverful" is a blessing; the children "round about the table" are supreme joy; and the consummation of human happiness in the peaceful evening of life is to see one's "children's children". To be childless is an irreparable tragedy.

Parents who determine to rear a family are taking the way of difficulty. It will mean a life of self-effacement and constant self-sacrifice; such complete concentration upon the interests of others that there will be no time left for thinking about themselves. But, oddly enough, that *is* the road to happiness. The basic argument, as has been noted, for the increase of the grounds for divorce is the right of people to be happy. Without admitting that there is any such right, it needs to be plainly said that happiness can never be found by seeking it or fighting for it. It is the most elusive of all things. Strive to win it and man will always fail; they that seek it shall *never* find it. But to forget all about it and to lose oneself completely in interest and concern for other people is a way of living which results surely in the inheritance of real satisfying happiness. This is not sentimentalising: it is sober fact.

The picture commonly painted of the harassed parents of a large family struggling to make both ends meet, worried with multitudinous cares and responsibilities is not so much untrue as out of perspective. It has thrown into the background, or omitted altogether, the never-failing and constantly increasing interest and delight in the up-bringing of children. The father who is "slaving" to provide for his children and the mother who is "pinching and scraping" to make both ends meet are infinitely happier than the couple next door who "can't afford" to have a family. Indeed, the prescription which a wise doctor might well give to the young married women, nominally suffering from "nerves", but who are really bored with chasing pleasure and with no interest in life but the fretful anxiety which is the nemesis of self-centred living, should be to obey the laws of nature and experience the all-absorbing interest of a family which will allow them no time to think about themselves.

So much has been said on the other side that no apology is offered for this emphasis upon the old-fashioned way of living. Is it for instance really true that the parents with the limited family of one or possibly two children, *are* doing the best for their offspring and giving them the best start in life and providing them with the best education for their success in after years? Is it true that the quality of such children is better than that of the family each one of which has had the discipline which only brothers and sisters can give? Is it true that the solitary child or the "pigeon-pair" are as happy as those who have grown up in the rough and tumble of a family? Has the solitary child learnt that independence of character which is the product of the community life of a family?

Beyond all question, the child has a right to a happy childhood, but that happiness is chiefly found in the companionship of his brothers and sisters, and in the discipline and "licking into shape" which only brothers and sisters can give, is found a character-training which nothing else can provide. It would be safe to wager that the children of *Mrs. Wiggs of the Cabbage Patch* know vastly more of the undiluted happiness of childhood than the precocious little old man or woman who is the solitary child, (sometimes pampered but often neglected) in the so-called "family" of the well-to-do parents who cannot "afford" more children because they want to do their "best" for such as they have and to give them "as good a start in life" as they had themselves. In fact, such parents are doing *none* of these things. Such children have never been young; the discipline of "give and take", the training in "keeping their own end up", which are the commonplaces of family life and by no means the least valuable things it offers, have never been their experience and when at last such young people find themselves compelled to face the world they have never learnt the elementary lessons which the member of a family imbibed in his earliest years. Whatever truth there may be in the argument that "quality is better than quantity", the quantity are in fact better, much better, in quality than solitary children.

We are envisaging the *Christian* home. Just as the grace of God is needful as the foundation of marriage, so also the grace of God alone can enable parents to create a Christian family. A married couple who undertake this task should realise that they are co-operating with God in doing the most wonderful thing within human reach, something in which they cannot succeed without the constant help of God. The Christian home cannot be built without the aid of the Christian Faith.

Far too little attention is paid to the wise injunction in our Prayer Book that the newly married couple "should receive the Holy Communion at the time of their marriage, or at the first opportunity after their marriage." The importance of the married couple sealing their love for one another by that act of Christian worship in which they seal their common love to Christ and consecrate to God the home they are beginning to create cannot possibly be over-stressed.

"I've prayed for you, my son, every day and night since you were born" (and then after a little pause and a quiet smile), "and indeed for many a day and night *before* you were born!" So said a Christian mother to her son; and so it should always be. The children of many prayers will seldom, if indeed ever, be unblest by God. Here again the Old Testament teaching was so sure and strong! The children were an "heritage and gift" from God and the responsibility of bringing them up in the faith and fear of God was the primary duty of the parents both by word and example.

When parents complain that their children are difficult, intractable and unresponsive, the question often asserts itself: "Have you ever given them a chance and shown them the best way?" For it can be confidently claimed that children who have been taught to pray by their parents, taught public worship by churchgoing parents, taught to kneel at the altar rails in companionship with father and mother will never be wanting in love and respect for their parents and in reverence for the faith practised and taught by those parents. In this, as in so many departments of life, Christianity has seldom been given a chance.

This is not the place for a detailed consideration of the economic problem occasioned by the large family. But one or two remarks must be made on this point, although the reluctance to produce a family is by no means entirely, or perhaps even mainly, due to poverty, for this alarming feature in our social life is much more frequently seen among the wealthy than in the poorer levels.

Nevertheless, the expense of rearing children is a grave deterrent not only among the artisans, but in those circles where the keeping up of appearances is regarded, and not altogether without good reason, as vitally necessary. If such people are expected to produce families of reasonable size, the State must recognise its duty towards them. It does not imply acceptance of the totalitarian view of the State to demand that the people who are facing the responsibility of producing and rearing the population without which the State itself could not exist have a right to receive such assistance as is needed from the public funds. To rear a family is to enrich society and instead of having to overcome all kinds of deterrents and face years of unnecessary financial anxiety such parents should receive family allowances in no way as an act of charity, but as a recognition by the State of invaluable services they are rendering to the whole community.

There is little doubt that a reform of this kind is near at hand, but there is another adjustment little less urgent. Theoretically, every child is able to climb the ladder of educational privilege but, in practice, it is only the few children of exceptional promise in the poorer strata of the community who are able to do this. It is unquestionable that the public school education loads the dice heavily in favour of the children of the well-to-do, and the demand for equality of opportunity in education for children of all classes is one which is becoming so insistent that even if there was the will to resist it there will not be the power to do so. Here again the intervention of the State will be necessary and rightly so for the State cannot afford to waste its greatest assets by neglecting to develop to the full the abilities of its children.

Finally, a word must be said upon the grave national situation which is rapidly coming to a head through the fall in the birth-rate. This is such a complicated and specialist subject that it is impossible to do much more than express a point of view.

The chief difficulty which confronts those who call for a consideration of the problem is the practical fact that very few people are able to concern themselves about a future which reaches further than the generation to which their children belong. The words of the President of the Obstetrical and Gynæcological Section of the Royal Society of Medicine in a letter to *The Times*, April 8th, 1942, express this well:

> Unfortunately no political party looks very far ahead or has much vision. That is left to small minorities who are designated "alarmists". Later, when the correctness of their views and warnings are confirmed, emergency measures are excitedly introduced and the minorities are then told that there must be no recriminations. . . . The situation will become desperate in some years' time, hurried legislation will then be too late . . . impending disaster is on our doorstep.

These are very grave words from a man of science. In the past fifty years the birthrate has fallen from 32 per 1,000 of the population to 14·1! Simultaneously, the length of life has increased and the prospect before us is that in another fifty years our population will have fallen by at least one third: we shall be a race of predominantly elderly people and worst of all it will then be too late to remedy the evil. Race extinction will stare our grandchildren in the face, for it has been reckoned that at the present rate the population of the British Isles will, in one hundred years, fall to under 5 millions.

In the correspondence in *The Times* to which reference has been made, it was pointed out that in a census made in 107 boys' public schools, it was revealed that 38·19 per cent of the boys were only sons and 20·51 were only children. The arguments advanced against larger families were very largely based upon the necessity to maintain the standard of living, the scanty leisure enjoyed by the mother of several children, the wrong scale of values which treated with "humorous or contemptuous references" the parents of large families. But there was one writer who struck the note which the Christian (and all sensible people) would re-echo: "The writers on the birthrate always make the production of children a dull affair. If someone could get up and shout out what fun it is to have a family, the young married people might listen."

It is manifest that in this, as in everything else, the Christian Faith points the way not only to happy and healthy living but to the way of wisdom. A nation which refuses to obey the age-old command "Be fruitful and replenish the earth" must be prepared to pay the penalty. We have no right to expect that the great unpopulated areas in Canada and Australia should remain ours if we persist in a "dog-in-the-manger" policy which would leave them thinly populated while other nations have not room in which to live. Race suicide will mean the ultimate end of the British Empire.

TOWN AND COUNTRY PLANNING

The Bishop of Chelmsford has explained the moral atmosphere essential if the home is to play its part in a Christian society. Mr. Trystan Edwards considers the ideal material setting for home life. After the war there will be an immense amount of building and re-building. Architects, town planners and the building trade operatives are all considering what sort of houses shall be erected and it is a matter for particular satisfaction that the workers are demanding that their skill and industry shall be employed in the construction of comely and comfortable homes, fit for the children of God to live in.

In his Gifford Lectures, His Grace the Archbishop of Canterbury declared that Christianity is the most materialistic of all the great world religions. It is concerned with the material surroundings of man's earthly life and it therefore regards the confinement of families in squalid, crowded ugliness as an offence to their Creator.

Mr. Trystan Edwards is a practical idealist. He not only knows what ought to be done, he knows how it might and should be done. He has thought out all sides of a difficult problem, and is ready with a plan, which is the more Christian because it is practical, the Christian being of all men most inclined to realism and least attracted by mere head-in-air sentimentality.

TOWN AND COUNTRY PLANNING

By A. Trystan Edwards

In *The Times* of April 1st, 1942, there appeared the following statement: "A town planning exhibition, organised by the Port of Portsmouth Chamber of Commerce, is shortly to be held in the nave of Portsmouth Cathedral at the express invitation of the Provost. A building which, as Portsmouth parish church, dates back to the twelfth century and which, as Portsmouth Cathedral, is being extended to meet the needs of the twentieth century, is a most suitable place to invite people to consider the plans which are being made for the new Portsmouth. This exhibition will be held with the concurrence of the Lord Mayor and Corporation of Portsmouth who have used the cathedral as their civic church for 700 years."

Two important conclusions can be drawn from the foregoing announcement: in the first place, the authorities of the church show themselves to be of opinion that the establishment of a Christian order is not possible without "physical reconstruction" of the right kind, and secondly, those for whom town planning is a major interest recognise the spiritual import of this activity, That the Church is now taking a live and practical interest in town and country planning was made extremely clear to the present writer, as he was privileged to attend a series of meetings convened by the Industrial Christian Fellowship with the object of putting forward, as a subject for discussion, a scheme of "physical reconstruction" which would give effect to the principles of social amelioration outlined at the Malvern Conference. The following subjects were placed on the agenda:

1. The question of the best method of housing and of whether we are compelled to be a nation of flat-dwellers.
2. The question of a possible check to the further expansion of urban areas.
3. The question of the balance between agriculture and industry.

In the course of the discussions it became apparent that the representatives of the Industrial Christian Fellowship were profoundly dissatisfied with recent tendencies in housing policy, believing that much of the rehousing undertaken in the inter-war period was wrongly conceived and that these mistakes require to be remedied even at the cost of a considerable amount of demolition. Secondly, they were united in urging the need for a comprehensive building programme for both towns and villages, to include not only housing but every type of structure which ministers to the spiritual and physical well-being of men, women and children. And, lastly, they were convinced that there should be a major redistribution of population in order to relieve the congestion in the larger industrial towns and also to facilitate the restoration of agriculture to its proper place in the national economy.

Three separate issues here seem to be involved, namely the art of civic design itself, the formulation of a definite scheme of national reconstruction in terms of town and country planning, and the technique of mass migration. A discussion of the topic first named will be concerned with general ideals of urban life, for it is obviously useless for a group of economists, statisticians and enthusiasts for hygiene to get together and produce arguments in favour of building a number of new towns, for instance, if at the same time the type of town these experts advocate fails to satisfy certain essential human needs, so that the people for whose benefit the new towns are planned resolutely decline to move into them. The second part of the argument will be an outline of a national scheme of building designed to solve our housing problems and to facilitate the conduct of our agriculture and industry, and will also deal with the financial arrangements which will need to be devised in order to implement such a scheme. The third section, devoted to determining the procedure of peopling the new towns with well-balanced social communities, will also have a wider significance inasmuch as it will be an exposition of the technique of mass migration in general. This matter not only concerns the welfare of the British Dominions overseas, some of which are now seriously under-populated, but also has a bearing upon international relations, for it may be found that organised migration may be one of the pre-conditions of a lasting peace.

Let us begin, then, with a brief examination of what we mean, or should mean, by town planning and civic design. It appears necessary first to reassert the principle, accepted by philosophers of all persuasions, that in the study of an important subject one must continually bear in mind the *whole* subject, if the parts are to be viewed in their true perspective. Town planning has suffered in repute through the activities of those who have concentrated their thoughts upon a single aspect of it. The so-called housing "experts" have perhaps been the worst offenders in this respect. On the one hand we have the fanatical exponents of "open development", a convention of building according to which rehousing must always assume the form of small detached units either in sprawling suburbs or in sprawling new towns; these people have such a horror of overcrowding that they go to the opposite extreme and would plant out human beings like cabbages on the countryside. In their passion for hygiene they omit to satisfy the human need for sociability. On the other hand we have the advocates of the tall blocks of tenements who talk learnedly about the relation of the cubic content of a building to the possible amount of open space surrounding it. To such theorists an open space is a mathematical abstraction, and they appear not to be aware that its value to human beings depends upon the degree of its accessibility! Moreover, they are completely unconcerned with the relation of these tall blocks to the pattern of the town as a whole. If it is suggested that the skyscrapers will put out of countenance the church and other public buildings in the town, the advocates of this kind of housing development are completely nonplussed, for the simple reason that they have never given a thought to some of the basic principles of civic design.

The capacity of urban architecture to enshrine a great civilisation is largely dependent upon the degree in which it can express, by architectural means, a certain scale of spiritual values. If, for instance, we are to assume that a church is really more important than an insurance company, then the church building, in the silhouette of any town, must actually be more prominent than is the structure erected to house the insurance company, and the upholders of the church should cause a regulation to be passed whereby not only insurance building but all commercial and domestic buildings should be kept reasonably low and, furthermore, should not take to themselves spires, towers, or domes of a kind traditionally associated with churches. And the architectural status of Parliament buildings, town halls, art galleries, opera houses and other structures of Governmental or cultural importance should be similarly safeguarded. There was a time when the common sense and good manners of those engaged in building development caused them to respect such a scale of civic values instinctively, but that was, of course, before the financial speculator became the principal executive power responsible for the erection of buildings and also before the theory of architecture had been obligingly modified to meet this situation by the "functionalists" who are content to ignore all considerations of design which are not "practical" in the narrowest sense of this word.

Yet it is extremely important to establish the relative degree of prominence which may justly be accorded to structures serving various purposes in a town. Indeed, the formulation of such a scale of values in terms of building is the highest, the most difficult, but at the same time the most fascinating intellectual task to which an architect can address himself. In replying to a question concerning the nature of government, Confucius is reputed to have said "Where the prince is prince and the minister is minister, where the father is father and the son is son, there is government." Likewise it might be said "Where the church is church, where the town hall is town hall, where the theatre is theatre, where the shop is shop, where the factory is factory, and where the private house is private house, there is civic architecture." The buildings must not only act their parts, but they must look their parts.

A compliance with the code just described results in both an inner harmony and a visible harmony in a town. Yet there is another element of spiritual import which requires to be introduced. As a principal object of planning towns is to bring people together for purposes of intercourse, a well-designed town should give formal expression to the Christian virtue of sociability. It may seem at first sight too simple and naïve a statement if it be suggested that the chief means whereby this object may be attained is the establishment of the street convention. Yet that buildings should touch one another on the right and on the left and should continue to hold hands, as it were, when they go round the corner of a street is a remarkably good idea, and there is no doubt that some of the most charming, the most beautiful and, it may be added, the most convenient towns in the world exemplify this convention.

The same principle finds expression not only in the great city but in the village, where, in England at any rate, we usually find that the centre of social life is a street of buildings in continuous formation. And what is such a delightful feature in these villages is that there is no class distinction expressed in the architecture; the houses of the agricultural labourers are cheek by jowl with those of the parson, the doctor, the lawyer, and the innkeeper, while the little shops are also aligned in close association with other buildings. It was not supposed that because land happened to be cheap in the locality, the houses should therefore be allowed to sprawl. Even if the land had been a free gift, an acknowledgment of the need for sociability would have resulted in the buildings being arranged in precisely the same configuration. *The forms of architecture should never be determined by the cost of land.* The conclusive argument against giving everybody a large garden in a town is not that the land in urban areas is too costly to admit of such an arrangement (for at some future date the land might be nationalised or the rent per square yard might be fixed at the same low rate all over the area under the jurisdiction of a municipal authority), but rather that it does not conduce to the convenience of the citizens if the size of the town is expanded in this way and that, moreover, such a dispersal of the houses militates against the achievement of that sociability which it is a principal object of a town to bring about.

The question may then be asked: "How close together should we place the buildings in a town?" The answer may very well be "As close together as possible," provided that there is also an insistence upon housing accommodation of a kind which safeguards the sanctities of family life and allows for the rearing of sufficient children to maintain and even to increase the birthrate, and provided also that the buildings are disposed in such a manner as to admit an adequate amount of sunlight and ventilation in the rooms. The widths of streets should be determined partly by this latter consideration and partly by the needs of traffic, it being borne in mind that two streets forty feet wide may carry actually more vehicular traffic, and with less inconvenience to pedestrians, than will one street eighty feet wide. A recommendation that every town should be as compact as circumstances allow does not mean that there should not occasionally be a large open space in front of important and noble buildings or pleasant residential squares with trees, or a sufficiency of playing fields or other recreational facilities, but that these desirable objects should be attained without waste of land and without destroying the dominant impression of continuous building which alone can give coherence to a town.

The two main principles of civic design which have just been expounded may be very briefly summarised as follows: the generality of buildings in a town should be kept fairly low in order that churches and other structures of special social consequence should be given the formal emphasis which is their due and spiritual and cultural values thus receive architectural recognition; and furthermore, the generality of buildings in a town should be in the street formation in order that human sociability may be encouraged. These principles are, in fact, observed in all the most admired towns both large and small whether on the continent of Europe or in our own country. By observing them, town planners can tread the popular middle way and avoid the errors committed by the two factions that may here be described as "the mounters" and "the sprawlers". The former conceive of new towns as groups of skyscrapers, each of which contains several thousand flats or offices. These dominate the town, and the other buildings take their chance—the town hall, deprived of its traditional architectural features and thus unrecognisable without a label, is nowhere in particular while perhaps the church is allowed to rear its little head in a corner.

This type of "model town" was illustrated in a popular weekly journal not long ago and held up to the admiration of its readers. Not only was it vulgar in conception but unpractical, for unlike the old-fashioned street formation which can be rebuilt bit by bit and adapt itself to necessary change as the years advance (and in so doing provide an historical record full of significance and fascination), these skyscrapers are incapable of organic growth and symbolise a completely static order of society. Even if it be assumed that the design expresses nothing more than a form of exhibitionism on the part of its authors and is not intended to be a serious attempt to solve any particular problem, its publication with uncritical comment cannot but do harm to the cause of civic design.

The "sprawlers" have been able to exercise a much greater influence upon the actual practice of town planning in this country than have the "mounters" because it is much easier to sprawl than to mount and the arguments in favour of sprawling are extremely plausible. The main cause of architectural sprawl is "open development". This type of layout, which was first sponsored by the protagonists of the Garden City movement, was intended to be a reaction against the long monotonous rows of the by-law streets which were characteristic of the Victorian period. The reformers, in their reaction against an admitted evil, formulated a new building code which may be described as an anti-street convention. This preference for architectural detachment was associated with a determination to give every householder a garden of a certain minimum size, and indeed an entirely new scale of values was established whereby the social status of a person was determined by the size of his garden and the distance his house was from the next house.

Residential areas laid out in accordance with the regulations formulated by these reformers decreed that the smallest houses in the scheme should be at twelve to the acre, houses of slightly better quality at ten to the acre, and so on, until we come to larger houses at six or four to the acre, and lastly there would be the habitations of the plutocrats, at perhaps only one to the acre. Thus it came to be considered by large numbers of people that the more sparsely houses were scattered over the landscape the more desirable they were.

At the present moment the severest critics of "open development" are the farmers who contend that this convention of building has resulted in an appalling waste of agricultural land.

Let us examine in detail the grounds for this complaint. Now, a very large part of the good agricultural land which has gone out of cultivation in the last twenty years is in the vicinity of existing towns and has now been subject to the encroachments of suburbia. It may be of interest, therefore, to make a rough estimate of the extent of this wastage of agricultural land, and also to define the causes of it in order that steps may be taken to guard against such a misdirection of building policy in the future.

In the case of rural areas in the neighbourhood of villages the maximum standard of density now permitted is six houses to the acre. Of the four million houses erected in Great Britain in the inter-war period it would be difficult to ascertain with any degree of exactitude the average density per acre of the houses, but it was certainly not more than eight to the acre, and may have been even less. It is not unreasonable to assume also that, but for these regulations, the average density of the four million new houses would have been not less than twenty-five to the acre, which allows for the establishment of a very high standard of housing accommodation. The amount of land thus wasted may not seem a large proportion of the total acreage of Great Britain, but when it is remembered that this land in the vicinity of existing towns included some of the best soil for market gardening in the whole country the loss seems to be a very serious one. And this calculation does not take into account the wastage of land which often occurs *between* the gardens of the houses in sporadic development on the ribbon roads or on the countryside, for very often in these localities good farm land is so cut up as to be almost useless. It has been estimated that a hundred houses scattered over a square mile of land can do much to render abortive all attempts to make the best use of it for agricultural purposes.

The foregoing considerations do but confirm the argument previously directed to establishing the main principles of civic design. It is now clear that the continuous street which was commended because it is the expression of human sociability has an additional justification inasmuch as by adopting it as the normal convention of building for all purposes the countryside will be preserved and the interests of agriculture will be safeguarded. What is now obviously required is a campaign to popularise the street house by showing that it can be so designed as to provide a twentieth-century standard of accommodation for people of all classes. The new street houses must offer such great attractions that people will gladly leave their villas on the ribbon roads and take up their residence in a town. In order that it may be legally permissible to build street houses of this kind, it will of course be necessary to amend certain building regulations which were framed by "experts" of Garden City persuasion with the precise object of enforcing the standardised "open development" favoured by them. These rules insist on very broad streets everywhere, with gardens in front of all the houses as well as at the back and, of course, a low density of the houses per acre even in the middle of a big town. The direct result of this latter ordinance is that when it is necessary to rehouse people in the built-up areas of our towns where land is very expensive the local authorities are obliged to erect blocks of tenements, although self-contained houses of good accommodation with plenty of light and ventilation in the rooms can be designed at similar densities per acre. So here we have the answer to Question No. 1 which was raised by the Town Planning Committee of the Industrial Christian Fellowship, namely "the question of whether we are compelled to be a nation of flat-dwellers."

In order to obviate the need to adopt the tenement form of dwelling all we have to do is to rescind the regulations which forbid the only practical alternative to it, which is the well-designed modern street house. By so doing, we should be conferring a great benefit not only on the wage-earners but on the middle classes as well, who have just as much right to family houses in the middle of a town.

A picture of the type of town to be aimed at has so far been sketched only in outline. Two main conclusions were reached, namely that spiritual and cultural values should be given architectural recognition by the traditional method of assigning formal pre-eminence to churches, the town hall and certain other specially important structures, and that the commercial and domestic buildings should be comparatively low, modest in their demeanour and, as a rule, disposed in continuous streets. And to this statement is now added a postscript to the effect that there should be no tenements for family occupation.

If the principles expressed in the formula are disregarded, the result is a vulgar town, an unsociable town, and a town which, by sprawling unnecessarily, inflicts an injury upon agriculture; and if, furthermore, the recommendation contained in the *addendum* to the formula, to the effect that there should be a veto upon the erection of blocks of tenements for family occupation, is likewise ignored, the birth-rate may decline so rapidly that there will presently be no need to build new towns or even to undertake any extensive remodelling of the existing ones, for the accommodation we already have will be more than adequate!

An attempt has been made to describe the main elements of architectural character and form in a town, but very little has yet been said about the details of planning for the satisfaction of twentieth-century needs. This is because an acceptance of the urban tradition which has here been analysed leaves not only architects but everybody else concerned with building development absolutely free to carry out any modern idea with regard to planning, construction, materials and stylistic treatment. New types of buildings can be introduced, serving new functions, there can be social centres, gymnasia, swimming baths, crèches, and playing fields galore, there can be scientific organisation of shopping facilities, industry and transport.

Two main principles could with advantage be exemplified in the plan of a modern town. The first is that the various functional zones, radiating from a civic centre, should be free to expand naturally and without the possibility of their being enclosed by other zones. The second principle is that in order to prevent the differentiation into zones from being too rigid, each zone should contain a subordinate civic centre in which a number of miscellaneous buildings might be situated, and these subordinate civic centres should be connected by a circular traffic route. A special feature of the town plan here recommended is that between some of the functional zones are green wedges of park reaching right up to the central nucleus of the town, and one of these green wedges would, of course, always be adjacent to a residential area. This arrangement is far superior to the so-called "green belt" around a town, for it enables the relationship of built-up area to recreational space to be retained even when a town expands.

In the residential zones there should be a number of shops for the supply of immediate household requirements. Places of worship, theatres, hotels, post offices and buildings fulfilling a number of other functions could be accommodated in any of the subordinate civic centres. By this means the necessary element of flexibility is introduced into the town plan without sacrificing the qualities of order and coherence. In the main civic centre the principal public buildings would be found. It is important that special provision should be made for the assemblage of the human crowd on pleasure bent. In this respect the "Garden Cities" are lamentably wanting—we see very wide roads and gardens galore but there is no place where the *crowd* is encouraged to foregather. In former times the populous streets did much to satisfy the gregarious instincts ·of town-dwellers, but to-day when motor traffic makes most of our streets unsuitable as places of concourse it is desirable to plan in every town a large social centre or bazaar where several thousand people can assemble under cover and where suitable entertainment, musical and other, can be provided.

It is calculated that a town of the kind here described, to

accommodate a population of 50,000, with a well-planned industrial area and exemplifying a high standard of housing for all, including 7 acres of playing field per 1,000 inhabitants, need occupy only one and three-quarter square miles, that is to say, a circle of one and a half miles diameter. There has here been described a twentieth-century town plan. But while it shows a number of novel features, there is no reason why the buildings should not comply with those time-honoured principles of civic design which have been outlined in these pages, that is to say, they should be disposed, for the most part, in the street formation, and neither "sprawl" nor "mount".

After this rather long preliminary architectural argument, it is possible to pass on to the second section of this chapter, which will deal with national reconstruction in terms of building. Reference has already been made to two important subjects raised at the Town Planning Committee of the Industrial Christian Fellowship, namely "the question of a possible check to the expansion of urban areas", and "the question of the balance between agriculture and industry". It was the unanimous opinion of the Committee that there was a serious maldistribution of the population in Great Britain, and that a measure of urban decentralisation was indicated. Unfortunately, however, decentralisation is not popular to-day because twenty years of compulsory "open development" in accordance with the Town Planning Acts has done much to spoil our countryside and at the same time has surrounded our towns with wide and dreary belts of villadom, the result of the notorious "twelve-to-the-acre" policy. Few people at the present moment want any more Garden Suburbs or even Garden Cities. In the future it will be possible to carry out a scheme of urban decentralisation on two conditions only; in the first place there must be an end to the convention of "open development" and any new towns which might be projected must be very compact indeed, or else the general public, heavily backed by the farmers, will veto the building of them. Secondly, the decentralisation from the big towns which, admittedly, is desirable for a number of reasons, must be accompanied by "centralisation" in the country areas, that is to say, some hundreds of thousands of small detached building units on the "ribbon roads" and elsewhere scattered over the landscape must actually be demolished and their occupants must be given alternative accommodation in compact new townships, and these townships collectively must occupy considerably less land than that which is now taken out of effective agricultural cultivation as a result of sporadic building development. A national scheme of building which complies with these

conditions was submitted to the consideration of the Town
Planning Committee here mentioned, and the proposals have
been elaborated in considerable detail in two leaflets published
by the Industrial Christian Fellowship.[1]

There is space here to give only a bare outline of the proposals.
The scheme involves the migration of five million people, i.e.
one-ninth of the population of Great Britain, to new towns each
of approximately 50,000 inhabitants. It is suggested that the
migrants should include:

2 million from London and its suburbs,

1½ million from other large towns,

1½ million from areas of sporadic development where several
hundred thousand ill-placed houses should be demolished.

Of the total amount of work involved in the scheme it is proposed that half should be allocated to existing towns and villages
and the other half to the new towns. In a twelve years' programme, the execution of which would cost £2,000 million, about
half the money expended on the scheme would be on land, roads,
factories, shops, public buildings, etc., and the other half on
houses, a million of which would be in the new towns and another
million in the existing towns. The amount of land required
would be less than one three-hundredth of the whole of Great
Britain. It is calculated that each of the new towns would save
England two hundred miles of "ribbon development".

When the bombardment is over, the first task will be to restore
and improve the existing towns. Some of the larger cities can
only be satisfactorily remodelled if ten per cent or more of the
inhabitants can be persuaded to migrate. The wartime evacuation schemes, however, should greatly aid in this process of
decentralisation by accustoming large numbers of people to seek
new homes. But the benefit would not only be confined to the
big cities, because £1,000 millions, fairly divided between all the
existing towns and villages in Great Britain, would admit of an
expenditure on new building works amounting to twenty-five
pounds per unit member of the population. Thus a town of
20,000 inhabitants would be entitled to an expenditure of
£500,000 (at pre-war rates for building costs) if it were to have
its proportionate share of the work which the building industry
is able to accomplish in the twelve years after the war. This is,
of course, on the assumption that during this period the other
half of the capacity of the building industry is employed on the
new towns.

[1] *New Towns for Old*, by the Rev. P. T. R. Kirk, price 3d. and *A Hundred New Towns
for Britain*, by A. Trystan Edwards, with an Introductory Essay by the same author,
on "The Place of Architecture in a Christian Community," price 6d.

After the latter are completed, the building industry would be free to continue whatever work is still needed to improve the existing towns and villages. The requirements of the bombed areas would, of course, receive first consideration, and a special building grant would need to be allowed for their benefit, thus diminishing to some extent the amount of building work which could be shared between the rest of the country during the initial period of the scheme.

It is considered desirable to design new towns rather than to add to small country towns or villages for the following four reasons. In the first place, by this means there is afforded a much needed opportunity to give absolutely free expression to the needs of our own age. Secondly, it takes less land to start *de novo* by designing a compact town than to add to the suburbs of the existing towns where the tradition of architectural sprawl has already been established. Thirdly, a method of decentralisation which took the form of adding from ten to twenty thousand people to small towns possessing a unique character of their own would be an act of vandalism. These charming old towns and villages are fitted to sustain only a moderate and natural growth and their social balance would be completely upset by a sudden large influx of population.

The scheme provides for seventy-five new towns in England, sixteen in Scotland and nine in Wales. A provisional siting of the new towns is suggested, but although a good deal of research has been expended upon this, the allocation of the towns to the various counties is put forward only as a subject for discussion, and the scheme does not stand or fall by any particular placing of the new towns. Naturally, the proposal takes account of the need to correlate all the facilities for transport whether by road, rail, inland waterways or by air. As might be expected, full use is made of the electric grid, and the majority of the towns would obtain power for industrial and other purposes from that source.

The Hundred New Towns scheme was formulated in 1933, and although it attained a considerable amount of publicity the proposals suffered from the disadvantage that they were submitted seven years too soon. There was little inclination at that time to consider a radical solution of the problems of town and country planning. Nevertheless, an Association was formed to promote the scheme, researches in connection with it were pursued with undiminished vigour, and in 1937 this Association was considered to be of sufficient importance for it to be invited to give evidence before the Royal Commission on the Geographical Redistribution of the Industrial Population. The Report of this Commission, which was issued in 1939, upheld the view, which has received emphatic confirmation since the beginning of the war, that a great many industries can quite easily be moved from one place to another. Some of the new concentrations of industry which have been brought about owing to the exigencies of war may be in localities suitable for the building of a modern town, but in most instances this will not be so, and it may be hoped that these war-time factories will not be retained on grounds of economy in places where the operatives cannot enjoy a civilised existence.

A few words more may here be said about the agricultural aspect of the scheme. Many thousands of the inhabitants of our large towns could only be persuaded to take up agricultural work if they were enabled to pursue this avocation without foregoing certain urban conditions of life to which they were accustomed. To such people the hundred new towns might make a strong appeal. The quarter of a million agricultural workers in these towns would be additional to the million or so, which is the present total of agricultural workers in the whole of Great Britain, and would be engaged in providing fresh vegetables and dairy produce for the inhabitants of the new towns. It is assumed, of course, that the main operations of agriculture would be conducted from the village centres as heretofore. The scheme would help to restore contentment to the inhabitants of rural areas, large numbers of whom would be within easy reach of the social services and recreational facilities which the new towns would provide.

The cost of the Hundred New Towns scheme would be no more than the money expended by this country in six months of the present war. The sponsors of the scheme do not attempt to specify the exact financial technique which should be adopted, but suggest that, as buildings are a unique security for money brought into being to finance them, it should be possible to carry out the scheme without the piling up of debt. Experience gained in recent months has helped to bring home the truth that the ability to provide the requisite labour and materials is the essential factor in all productive work. Thus it will be sufficient if the programme here proposed is related to the resources of the building industry. The principal question is not how much money will be available but how many "man hours" will be available when the building industry is working at full pressure.

The relation of "man hours" to building is here expressed in the formula that one "man hour" produces, on the average, five cubic feet of building. If an operative works 2,000 hours in a year, he can be responsible for 10,000 cubic feet, the equivalent of one cottage of value £500, at one shilling per foot cube. Should this average rate for building work, which prevailed

before the war, be exceeded, then the total cost of the scheme
would be more than the estimate of £2,000 millions, but the
extent of the programme is assessed in terms of realities, namely
the labour and materials available and not in terms of a fluctu-
ating value of money. It is assumed, however, that the Government will be successful in preventing a degree of monetary
inflation such as would result in a considerable increase in
building costs. A programme involving the expenditure of
£1,000 millions on existing towns and villages, and another
£1,000 millions on the new towns is well within the capacity of
the building industry to accomplish in a period of twelve years.
After the completion of the new towns, the major part of the
resources of the building industry would be devoted to the further
remodelling of the existing towns, some of which have long-term
policies such as might take thirty or more years to execute.

The scheme here outlined, whether or not it be accepted in all
its details, at least defines the scale of the programme of building
which should be undertaken if the English people are to enjoy
a healthy convenient and dignified urban life and if, furthermore,
the best arrangements are to be made for the conduct of our
industry and agriculture. While in discussions on national
planning it is often assumed that the essential preliminary step
is to create a Central Planning Authority, an opposite view is
here advanced, namely that the exact functions and statutory
powers of such a body should not be settled until after a national
plan has been formulated and endorsed by public opinion, for
the character and scale of the plan must determine the nature of
the administrative agency which is to carry it out.

If, for instance, the Hundred New Towns scheme were accepted,
certain legal, administrative and financial changes immediately
suggest themselves. In the first place the existing town planning
regulations would require to be modified in order to make
possible a return to the street formation of building, for, strange
as it may seen, at the present moment, it is actually illegal to
build compact new towns—we may only build Garden Cities in
"open development". Next, there should be a measure of
equalisation of railway rates for goods traffic in order that industries migrating to the new towns should not be handicapped
when competing with industries which have the advantage of
being nearer to London or to any other large market for manufactured goods.

Then, of course, there would need to be a new financial and
administrative technique which would ensure that a building
programme is limited only by the capacity and resources of the

building industry and not by a shortage of gold or of certain little bits of paper. One feature of the new dispensation would be that when in the course of reconstruction it is necessary to pull down any particular building, its owner should receive compensation not in terms of money to be spent as he pleases, but in the form of another building of equal cubical capacity on a site offering advantages not inferior to those of the original site. The problem of "compensation", which now presents such difficulties, would thus be immensely simplified. One of the tasks of a Central Planning Authority would be the final choosing of the sites of the new towns after all the relevant considerations had been taken into account, and the organising of a national system of transport in which roads, railways, inland waterways and aerial routes will be related to the revised urban pattern which will result when the new towns are built.

Whatever scheme of national reconstruction be ultimately adopted in this country, it would obviously be unwise to start planning any new roads or making out schedules of work for the building industry until such time as the Government has decided to what extent it wishes to commit itself to a policy of urban decentralisation. Its reluctance to make any pronouncement on this important issue is not due only to the circumstances of war because a similar indisposition so to do was shown by all the Governments which came to power in the twenty years preceding the war. The real reason for this, it is here suggested, is that the bureaucrats had not worked out the procedure which needs to be adopted if several million people are to be moved to new townships.

This brings us to the third part of the present chapter, which is concerned with the technique of mass migration, an extremely important element in town and country planning, for upon it depends the capacity of statesmen to correct serious maldistribution of population whether within the confines of a single state or in the world as a whole. For this reason the present writer makes no apology for devoting so much space to an exposition of the Hundred New Towns scheme. Even if, owing to the power of obstructive vested interests or through any other cause, not one new town was built in England as a result of it, the scheme would still merit some attention inasmuch as it represents the first serious attempt to evolve a twentieth-century technique of mass migration.

For a migration scheme four things need to be determined—the size of the new towns, the type of plan for the new towns, the procedure of building the new towns and the actual peopling of the new towns. Now there is an obvious justification for the thousand or more existing towns and villages in Great Britain being of different sizes because they were founded at different times and have numerous different social origins. But where a number of townships are brought into being by a single migration scheme, no such excuse for variation of size exists. The proposed act of colonisation must be conceived as a single act, because a great effort of national will is required to carry it out within a limited space of time. A certain homogeneity in the new towns would be a legitimate expression of their common origin and the common and collective purpose which they are called upon to fulfil. The task of organising the migration will only be of manageable dimensions if the new towns, at least when they start on their careers, are all of approximately the same size and of approximately the same internal constitution and exemplify the same type of plan which should result in their all possessing a certain minimum number of good qualities which few towns have possessed before. It should be almost a matter of indifference to the migrants which town they go to. Otherwise they would all want to flock to certain favoured towns, while the remainder might be neglected.

Next, the town plan itself must be especially designed for the mechanism of mass migration. The idea, not uncommonly held, that a population of about twenty thousand people might suitably be added in a short space of time to any existing town anywhere is quite untenable. The plan must be, in the true sense of the word, organic; that is to say, as it grows it must continue to maintain the right relationship between its various functional zones. Such a type of town plan has already been here described. Then, in order that the town should be habitable and sufficiently attractive, *before* the first migrants are invited to take up residence in it, all the buildings—churches, houses, schools, shops, factories, etc., for a population of at least 5,000, should be completed. There would thus be a social nucleus of the expanding town, which would help to direct the life of the new community. Perhaps, with increased experience in this technique of mass migration, it might be possible to complete a town for 50,000 people with every building perfectly fulfilling its function and with the inhabitants so carefully chosen that they can all march into the town at the same time and immediately begin to pursue their appointed avocations. That, of course, would be almost a miracle of organisation, yet not impossible of achievement some time in the future. It is necessary not only that the buildings themselves should be in the right numbers and of the right kinds but that among the people also all classes and occupations should be adequately represented. If the latter object is to be attained, a "migration pool" must be established, that is to say, a selected number of people from the areas which it is desired to evacuate, and this "pool" should include industrial workers, agricultural workers, schoolmasters, doctors, shop-keepers, laundrymen, window-cleaners, and so on. Then there should be an orderly programme whereby these people are sent to the new towns in the right proportions so that collectively they will constitute well-balanced social communities.

Naturally, the carrying out of such a plan is not an easy matter, but neither is the composing of an opera easy, nor a mastery of the theorems of higher mathematics, nor the organisation of a great military campaign. Yet it has never been argued that such tasks should not be attempted merely because they are difficult. With regard to mass migration we should ask whether in any particular circumstance it is desirable. If we obtain an affirmative answer to this question, it behoves us to take steps to make such a policy practicable. The researches in connection with the Hundred New Towns scheme were directed to this end.

It is important to remember that new towns may be needed not only when it is desired to move a population, but when it is desired to bring about a notable increase in population. In a letter to *The Times* of April 15th, 1942, Lord Bledisloe expressed the opinion that "Empire building without human bricks is an obvious impossibility and definite Governmental stimulus to their production is surely preferable to the stimulus to foreign aggression afforded by several million square miles of unoccupied terrestrial space, overfloated by the Union Jack." The "human bricks", however, require an accompaniment of ordinary architectural bricks, if there is to be migration on a large scale to the Dominions overseas. What here seems to be called for is a comprehensive plan, not merely an economic plan but an architectural plan, that is to say a definite scheme for the new housing accommodation and, indeed, the new towns which would be required, were our statesmen to take effective steps to bring about a rise in the birth-rate. The formulation of an ambitious plan, the fulfilment of which would be a symbol of an increased national power and vitality, would itself tend to inspire that mood of optimism and faith in the future which men and women need above all else if they are to undertake the duties of parenthood. And it stands to reason that when there is conspicuous architectural preparation beforehand for the reception of a continually increasing number of children, there is far more likelihood that the desired children will be born.

We need to ask ourselves, "What is the minimum population

3

which the British Commonwealth of Nations should aim at if it
is to appear obviously entitled to its vast territorial estate?" In
reply to this question, it is here suggested that it would be reasonable in the first instance to plan for a total population of ninety
millions, all of British descent, of which forty-five millions would
still be resident in Great Britain, twenty millions in Canada, five
millions in South Africa, and twenty millions in Australia and
New Zealand. When we bear in mind the cultivable areas and
the natural resources of these Dominions, the programme appears
reasonable. It represents an increase of about twenty-five
millions, that is to say, nearly forty per cent in the white population of the British Commonwealth. History shows that in former
times the population of England actually doubled itself in far less
than a hundred years. It has been calculated that an average of
four surviving children per marriage would cause the population
to be multiplied seven times in a century. So a plan to increase
the population by forty per cent in, say, thirty years, is not an
extravagant one—if the will to procreate is present, and if there
is money to pay for the children and accommodation for the
children.

We may pass over the financial issue, for it need not be supposed that the "scarcity economics", which have been the
cause of widespread poverty not only in the Dominions but in
Great Britain itself during the last twenty years, will be allowed
to hold sway after the present war.

Let us then consider the architectural aspect of the large-scale
migration which is now contemplated, and try to assess the
capacity of the building industry to cope with a programme of
work far greater than that entailed in the Hundred New Towns
scheme. Now, it will be remembered that, in the case of the
latter it was proposed to spend £2,000 millions in the course of
ten years, or £200 million a year. But according to figures
published by the Building Industries National Council, based on
the 1930 census, an annual expenditure of £600 millions on
building work would be quite normal. So the industry could
take the Hundred New Towns scheme in its stride very easily
indeed, and, in addition, have a considerable margin for "current
repairs". It is assumed that even if a migration scheme to the
Dominions is planned, the hundred new towns would still be
needed in Great Britain in order to redistribute the population,
and to make up for the existing shortage of houses and other
buildings which are urgently needed to minister to the well-being
of the present inhabitants. If we assume, as we may, that the
building industry in Great Britain alone could undertake another

hundred and fifty million pounds worth of work a year, that would
be equivalent of £4,500 million worth of building in thirty years
for the benefit of the Dominions overseas. This means, of course,
that part of the building industry in Great Britain would need
to migrate to the Dominions to supplement that in the Dominions.
Between them the task of carrying out a programme of £5,000
million worth of building, the equivalent of 500 towns of 50,000
people each should be easy of accomplishment, and, indeed,
there might be energy to spare to give a hand in India. An
imaginative scheme of reconstruction in that country, in the
execution of which British engineering skill were allied to native
Indian craftsmanship would perhaps do more to put an end to
political acerbities than can the framing of new constitutions.

Needless to say, the "plan for the British Commonwealth of
Nations" is here put forward only tentatively, just to state a
problem and to indicate that it is not insoluble. A comprehensive plan, whatever it might be, would, of course, need to be
approved by a Conference of Representatives of Great Britain
and the Dominions overseas. It is here suggested, however, that
it is by no means too soon for organisations or individuals to
make a start with the researches which the formulation of such
a plan would entail. Such "unofficial" plans should be thoroughly
canvassed before the calling of the Conference, which obviously
cannot perform its function unless it has an informed public
opinion behind it.

The technique of mass migration, as has already been hinted,
has an international aspect. The maldistribution of population
in the various continents was undoubtedly one of the factors
which brought about the present war. There are causes of
conflict between one country and another which can only be
removed by adopting a migration policy. But such a solution
will not suggest itself to statesmen unless an understanding of the
science of town and country planning is considered to be a
necessary part of their intellectual equipment. They should be
familiar with the means whereby transfers of population, instead
of being carried out under conditions of duress and cruelty, as
has too often been the case, may be accomplished in a civilised
manner to the manifest advantage and with the consent and
goodwill of the peoples concerned. This town and country
planning, when allowed its full scope, not only brings increased
contentment and well-being to the citizens of individual states,
but has a bearing upon foreign affairs and might even contribute
to the establishment of a lasting peace.

RELIGION IN THE SCHOOL

Again to quote the Malvern Report: "Every child should have the opportunity of an education till years of full maturity, that is to say including vocational training when desired, even to the age of eighteen, so planned as to allow for his peculiar aptitudes and for their full development, and to enable him to discover and fulfill his personal vocation in right relationship with Nature, Man and God. Opportunities for technical training are included in this conception of education and the importance of home environment is to be borne in mind. Education should throughout be inspired by a conviction of the supremacy of spiritual values."

RELIGION IN THE SCHOOL

By Hugh Lyon, the Headmaster of Rugby

Schoolmasters oscillate between two unhappy extremes, that of impatient conviction that they are making much fuss for nothing, striking perpetually at ghosts which are as the air invulnerable, and that of pontifical assurance that they are moulding the future of mankind. In the latter mood all that they do seems to be important, as any member of any scholastic conference will testify. Yet when we remember the competing influence of family, of friends, of city street, of books and talk and films; when we contemplate the all-important formative years which have done their work before we even see a boy, and then look ahead to the maturity which awaits him, fifty years or more against our four or five; when finally we realise how little the teaching side of his school life seems to count compared with the rest of it, and even in that how bottomless his capacity for forgetfulness; then we may well be forgiven for abandoning all claim to any influence whatever, being convinced not of the importance of our efforts but of their impotence.

But to despair is a betrayal of our trust. It is one of the most comforting (and at times the most frightening) facts about life that no man can ever tell how much or how little he has influenced his neighbour. There are moments in life when we are inordinately receptive, when a chance word or action may influence us for years or for ever; these moments come for the most part in youth, and it is as often as not the teacher who sows the fruit-bearing seed. He may never know it, certainly he cannot plan it. But he can never assume that anything he says or does, officially or privately, in the presence of the young will pass into oblivion; and that should make him a very prayerful and a very humble man.

This exordium is intended to anticipate the obvious criticism which will occur to most of those who read on. It is impossible to talk about religion and religious teaching in the school without the implication that they *matter* immensely; and it would be misleading as well as, I think, unjust if such an assumption were to be taken as a sign of self-importance. In a subject of such far-reaching consequence every influence which is brought into play must be examined and shaped with the utmost care. Teachers know well enough that each particular thing they do may be, for good or ill, without permanent effect. But it may not.

Religious education is a stage in a process and nothing more; an obvious fact, but one which is sometimes forgotten in the closed atmosphere of school life. We should be laying or strengthening foundations, not turning out finished products. This means that we must be on our guard against compiling schemes *in vacuo*; there must be constant cross-references not only to the contemporary atmosphere of home and friends but also to the institutions and standards into which our pupils will one day emerge. We must fit them—not *for* that world (that suggests a conformity which is not necessarily desirable) but to live in that world. Somehow or other we must give them the spiritual equipment to encounter situations which lie beyond the microcosm of school life, though in these days rumours of them penetrate even the most cloistered academy. So it is not out of place to preface a discussion of religion in the school with a brief survey of the main tendencies in the world outside.

We still call ourselves a Christian nation, and there would be general indignation if anyone in authority failed to pay lip-service to the faith of our fathers. The indignation would be sincere, but it would be for the most part instinctive and not intelligent; for "Christianity" has weakened steadily in meaning, and nowadays seldom implies more than a general approval of the ethical ideas which we inherit from Western civilisation. This will at once become evident if for "Christianity" we substitute "the Christian church"—a substitution which would at one time have been taken for granted. At once we shall find dissension where before there was unthinking unity. There are perhaps not over-many agnostics and atheists in England; but there are probably even fewer who would call themselves churchmen, or who show their churchmanship by attendance at public worship. For the rest there is a vague belief in some kind of God and in the superiority of Christian to pagan ideals, and a profound distrust of all religious movements and organisations. There is a blurring of outlines, a reluctance to accept any doctrine as inescapably true, a questioning of everything which claims to be of universal validity. This tendency has perhaps been accentuated by two major wars, but it is not due to them. Science has made havoc of so many certainties that it has brought certainty itself under suspicion; and relativity has escaped from the physical world where it is no doubt as true as it is, to the layman, incomprehensible and invaded other spheres where it can be readily understood and is altogether false. There is a serious revolt, led by some who should know better, against the "absolutes", against objective standards of truth and order and beauty and virtue. Convention and tradition vary with the centuries, and those values which they express in changing form are held to be subject to the same variation. And the world as a whole tends to echo in all seriousness Hamlet's mockery: "There is nothing either good or bad but thinking makes it so."

The advance of science has had also another important, if more indirect, effect on men's faith. We have become accustomed to miracles, so perpetually confronted with new inventions that we have lost the faculty of wonder. While we are safely past the false conflict between evolution and the book of Genesis, we are in the middle of a graver crisis, which this time seeks not to contrast divine revelation with scientific truth but to harmonise them; to equate the miracles of the Gospels with the miracles of gramophone and wireless; to "explain" the former as the latter are known to be explicable, and so by implication to empty religion of its supernatural element. And what place is there then in man's life for Christ, the Son of the Living God? Humanism, in one form or another, is really the working faith of a number of men and women who still imagine themselves to be Christians. Men are thinking more and more in purely human terms about themselves and their destiny. They are losing interest in a God who seems to have lost interest in them, and in a church which is divided against itself and either unable or unwilling to stand out against the forces of evil.

It is not surprising that this loss of religious conviction has been accompanied by a lowering of the moral standard. It is one thing to try to live as in the sight of God, and to base one's treatment of one's fellow-man upon the conviction that we are all children of one Father, all "brothers for whom Christ died". It is another to rely upon conventions of decent behaviour which are continually and it seems successfully flouted both in the nation and in the world at large. If we will not postulate absolute standards of morality we must be prepared to see them steadily deteriorate. The "natural" virtues of courage, endurance and sacrifice can be (and are being) used to attain the vilest ends; no superfluity of such "human" excellence can atone for a deficiency in the fruits of the spirit.

Now if the outside world is like this, then inevitably the families of most of our pupils will be affected by the same virus; still more the factories and workshops into which many of them will go. What then is the school to do? It is often urged not to persist in maintaining an "artificial" atmosphere of worship and doctrine, which corresponds to nothing in the child's home surroundings; this, it is suggested, will only result in the whole school atmosphere being tainted with an unreality which will make it worthless as a preparation for life. At the worst, everything connected with school and school training will be impatiently and indignantly discarded, including not only the practice of religion but those moral standards which have been closely linked with it. At the best there will be bewilderment and tension, a constant tug-of-war between the dictates of authority and the trend of modern thought.

This sounds good sense; but such arguments rest upon two assumptions which we have no right to make. In the first place, the picture of modern tendencies of thought given above is manifestly incomplete. The two wars may have disturbed many who sat loosely to their faith, but they have wrought still greater havoc with the conviction (common at the end of the last century) that man was progressing happily under his own steam towards the millennium. It is surely humanism and not religion which has been found wanting. What is stirring in men's minds to-day is not so much an impatience with tradition—that is stale news now—but a quest for some dry ground on which their feet may rest, some certainties to replace those they have discarded. The house is swept and garnished, and there is anxious search for a tenant to hold it against the devils which have overrun so many hearts in Europe. Hence the clamour for new truth, a new order, a new god; may it not be the duty and the privilege of the schools of to-day to reveal through their members the nature of that truth and that order and that God? It would not be the first time in the history of Christendom that the sun (the same sun) has shone out in new brilliance from the clouds which had obscured it.

But even if this diagnosis be false there is a second reason why we should teach the Christian faith. We must not let the mists of controversy hide from us the essential fact that we are concerned not with what is desirable or convenient but with what is right and true. If the Christian revelation is a delusion, then no doubt the world will in due time sweep it and us into limbo. But if it is true it is the supreme truth, and only at the peril of our souls do we ignore or belittle it or fail to teach it to those placed in our charge. We may, indeed we should, do what we can to bring its presentation into line with modern thought and to link it with the social and national life of the world to-day. But we must assert its fundamental truth for this age as for all others. There can be no compromise there. If all the world had drifted into agnosticism, then our duty would be not to conform and teach others to conform, but to strive the more fervently to stem the evil tide. Morality, whether personal or national or international, will never for long resist the appeals of self-interest unless it is founded upon faith; and for the Christian teacher the only foundation is faith in the Redeemer of mankind, who by His death upon the Cross has bridged the gulf between sinners and their God.

We therefore approach the question of the form which religious education should take in our schools with a firm conviction that it is both right and necessary, and with a refusal to be daunted by the feeling of impotence which so often overcomes us. We have further established two things; first, that our teaching and practice must be kept in constant touch with the world and the church outside the school; and secondly, that we have to instil convictions which will be proof against all the influences which may be brought to bear against them, and for the most part to do this with no active help from home teaching or atmosphere.

Religious education in this context means more than ethical education; it must be something which can be called Christian. On the other hand it does not mean sectarian education. I shall discuss later on the place of doctrine; but it should at the outset be stated that the allegation that the movement for more thorough and systematic education in religion is a plot to capture the child for this or that denomination is quite untrue. Its aim is really threefold and it approaches it in three ways. Two of these are the formal teaching and worship which find a place in the school time-table. The third is less tangible but more pervasive, a spirit which should inform the whole life of the school and its members. Just as through worship we seek to create a sense of Christian fellowship and membership of the church, and through teaching try to reveal the main content of the Christian faith, so in all kinds of ways, official and unofficial, we should be encouraging the practice of Christian virtue. This is perhaps the hardest part of our task, since it depends not on what we do or say but on what we are; but it is also that part which is almost universally recognised as necessary. So I shall say something of it first before going on to more controversial matters.

The difficulty about the Christian ethic, as it is stated in the Gospels, is that it is both adult and uncompromising. It is expressed in vivid terms which appeal forcibly to the young, but its meaning is sometimes hidden in phrases which are all but repugnant to them. We who are older believe that we know what is intended by meekness, turning the other cheek, loving our enemies, and going two miles when forced to go one. We can see there ideals of great value and difficulty. But these injunctions seem not only incongruous but unmanly to the boy in the rough-and-tumble puppy stage. And Christ, who so loved children, would have been the last to impose on them a smug precocity or a self-righteous abstention from the hurly-burly of the school playground. This is a crude instance of what I mean, and few teachers will go wrong about it; but in our own familiarity with Christ's teaching we may not realise how literally it may be interpreted at first hearing; with the result that children sometimes form and retain an altogether false idea both of the teaching and the Teacher. To some extent the work of interpretation will come into the school lesson; but it is not there that Christian ethics are really taught, nor even from the pulpit, though they are there more in place. It is by our own attitude to them and to each other, by our unremembered words and acts of kindness or jealousy or selfishness or love, by all that part of our lives which they know to be real because they only get informal glimpses of it, that our pupils will judge us and the worth of our Christian exhortations. The roughest and most backward school can be instinct with the spirit of loving-kindness, of generosity, of simple honesty, of unhesitating self-sacrifice; and it will then be a place of Christian education. But no scripture schemes or chapel services or conventional gentility will make a Christian community of a school where relations between its members are narrow and envious and embittered. "If we live by the Spirit, by the Spirit let us also walk."

This matter of Christian atmosphere is so important that it has been accepted by the lazy-minded and those who are scared of religious controversy as being all that is necessary. But without the foundation of doctrine and worship it is as the house built upon sand. In fair weather it will stand the test, and the genial influence of school has inspired many a placid life with ideals of unselfishness and good nature. But when trouble comes a man must draw from deeper wells than these. If he has learnt his conduct by rote and his ethics at second-hand, where is he to find the strength to maintain them in the face of attack? It is our duty to give our pupils more than this; to teach them the faith which has, from the Roman arena to the German concentration camp, upheld its followers through torture and through death, and to enrol them, by the practice of worship, in the fellowship of the universal church.

Before we consider these two more formal elements of religious education, it is only right to defend the schools against accusations which are too readily brought against them. There must be very few schools, inside or outside the national system, where no attempt is made to give some kind of religious instruction. Unfortunately the Archbishops' letter, which was intended to encourage good work already being done and free it from the handicaps which fetter it, was widely interpreted as an accusation of neglect. At once all those who felt uneasy at the deteriora-tion of moral standards felt they could now blame our "pagan national schools", and there was a chorus of solemn admonition to teachers to start doing what most of them had been doing for many years past. It would indeed be truer to say, with critics of another order, that the schools had for some time been striving to implant in their pupils habits and ideals which were at marked variance with those of their homes. It must be rather galling for a teacher who has for ten years been watching his children un-learning at home every evening and all through the long holidays those elements of religion he has striven to teach them to be urged by writers to the Press to turn his thoughts to religious education. Most of what is discussed hereafter is already taking place on a wide scale. School-teachers are, as a body, more inclined to religion than any other lay community; if they are given guidance and help we can trust them a long way. The main problem, as we shall see, lies elsewhere.

To pass to the question of worship. Most schools, elementary and secondary, have a daily "assembly", at which they begin their school day with a rededication of themselves and their com-munity to the service of God and ask for His blessing on the coming day. There is usually nothing in this short service which could be called violently sectarian, and it is normally attended by all the children (except those who miss it habitually because of a faulty bus or train service), though here as elsewhere parents have of course the right of "contracting out". For the great majority of schools this is where worship begins and ends; is there anything further that can be done to increase the value and meaning of this side of religious education?

First of all we should, I think, welcome the fact that the practice is so widespread, and commend it strongly to those Headmasters and Headmistresses who do not at present observe it. Naturally its value depends immensely upon the way the service is taken, on the personality of the Head and on the atti-tude towards it of other members of the staff. It may be a mere matter of routine, perfunctory and almost meaningless, without any appeal to the child's spiritual awareness, and used more for giving out notices and getting the runners punctually to the tape than for worshipping God. It can become very much more— not by being twisted into the expression of personal eccentricity, but by a reverent and sincere offering of prayer and praise as if they really mattered, and by instruction from time to time in the place of worship in the church.

On the first of these points we need say little; but it does raise the vexed question of the obligations of the Headmaster or

Headmistress. It is one of the essential points in the teacher's charter of freedom that no teacher shall be handicapped or victimised because of his or her religious opinions. This is in harmony with our tradition of liberty, and with two qualifications there is no reason why the most fervent advocate of religious education should quarrel with it. The first qualification is an obvious one, which will meet us when we discuss the subject of religious teaching; it is that no teacher should be engaged for any post which necessarily involves the teaching of scripture unless he is both competent and willing to teach it. What these much-discussed adjectives mean we shall consider in due course. The second qualification is more controversial. Headships are naturally enough the plums of the teaching profession, and to demand that candidates for such posts should be practising Christians raises in acute form the old "Religious tests for teachers" question on a higher plane. But the issue is funda-mental and must be faced. For if we are right in asserting that in a professedly Christian country children in all schools should be above all else instructed in the substance and practice of the Christian faith we must satisfy ourselves that this primary purpose is not defeated through lack of guidance and conviction in Head teachers. To delegate so vital a task to another is to cause doubts at once in the pupils' minds, to the detriment either of their school or their faith. Should it not be regarded as part of the necessary equipment for those aiming at the highest posts in our schools that they should be ready to support, with sincerity if not with enthusiasm, the spiritual education offered there? If they cannot do this, then have they not been mistaken in their am-bition? I know how grave are the objections to so drastic a change in our habits of thought and practice. Clearly there have been many great teachers and administrators in the scholastic profession who have made capable Heads of schools and have yet not subscribed to the Christian faith. I know too how such a restriction might well induce a hypocrisy and bogus religiosity in ambitious teachers which would be much more undesir-able than honest agnosticism. But the questions remains, and it must be answered. If this really is the most important element in education, then how can the Head of a school stand aside?

The second way in which I suggested that a child could be helped to make the most of the periods of worship was by instruc-tion. The impulse to worship may be natural, but it needs guidance; and the ritual of worship needs explanation. To-day so many think of worship (when they think of it at all) as the way in which various sects express their points of difference that it is necessary to point out how from the beginnings of the church worship was the expression of its unity. Man was made to glorify God and enjoy Him for ever, and it was in the daily or weekly gatherings of the church that he sought to satisfy this need. Christianity never was and never could have been a purely personal religion; it was from the first the faith of a community. And it is on the expression of this faith in communal worship that its strength has always rested. Persecution has never driven Christians apart from one another; whether in Roman catacomb, on Scottish hillsides or in German cellars, they have always come secretly together, forced by their adversity to affirm still more strongly their need to worship, and strengthened by that worship to endure. It is hard to see in our languid and infrequent church-going any trace of that compelling power. Yet God is still among his faithful when two or three are gathered together, and if there is to be in truth a revival of the Church it will be both inspired by and reflected in the congregations in our churches. Children have a lively sense of tradition; and few will fail to respond more earnestly to the demands of a school service if they have been shown how the very words they utter are rich with the piety of countless generations, and how beyond and behind them there is the vast communion of the saints in every age with whom they are fellow-worshippers.

It is of first importance that school worship should be in harmony with that which most of the congregation will find in the churches they attend elsewhere; special school forms of service should be the exception and not the rule. Well-meaning attempts to make the service original and interesting not only defeat their own object once the first bloom is off them but— still more fatal—blur the essential continuity between school assembly and the worship of the church. This continuity can often be strengthened by occasional Sunday services (in day schools) to which pupils are invited with their parents. But even when the school meets alone and as a self-contained community it must never be forgotten. Here as elsewhere we must remember that we do but lay foundations, and that we are part of a wider whole to which our allegiance is due.

Boarding schools have problems and opportunities of their own, of which this is not the place to speak; not only because it would be difficult to do so except at length, but because conditions vary so much from one school to another that it is hard to formulate principles which are universally applicable. I propose therefore to pass to the question of teaching, about which there has been much discussion and little agreement.

It is difficult in a single article not to be dogmatic, and much of what I say on this subject will not necessarily command general assent. But it can at least serve as a basis for argument. It will at any rate be generally agreed that both in content and presentation our teaching must vary with the mental age of the pupil. There are many shades of variation, but the scheme suggested below adopts three main classifications; the primary stage, up to the age of 10 or 11; the secondary stage, from 11 to 15 or 16; and the post-certificate stage, for those who stay on at school after the first school examination. For all these groups elaborate and valuable schemes of instruction are available, and can be consulted; what I am going to discuss here is emphasis rather than content; advance in education is due as much to a change of emphasis as to an enlargement in scope or in material.

The first stage is the stage of story-telling. The lovely tales of the Old Testament, strung together on a single thread of the age-old purpose and promise of God, are fit matter for any youthful imagination. Glimpses can be given too of some of the prophets and of the psalmists; but for the most part it will be plain narrative, a long line of patriarchs and kings and deliverers, until the story sinks into the obscurity of the captivity and the more confused annals of the return from exile. Against this pageant of centuries we have balanced the story of the gospels, the chronicle of three years of a single life. But even at this stage we must observe proportion and not leave the children looking on the Old Testament and the New Testament as two strangely dissimilar halves of a single apple. "Progressive revelation" is an alarming phrase, but the meaning of it is not beyond the conception of a child of eight. And we must guard even at this stage against the headaches which come from the attempt to harmonise Abraham's Jehovah with the Father of Jesus Christ. As the gospel story is unfolded the earlier history should be allowed to slip into the background where it belongs; a background without which the story would have been very different, but a background none the less. And the deathless figure of the God who taught and healed among men and went to torture and death for their sake will stand out in all its simplicity and beauty, drawing the eyes and the love of children to-day as He did two thousand years ago in Galilee. There is little if any need here of formal doctrine. The teacher has but to let the story tell itself, with a minimum of comment and interpretation.

In the secondary as in the primary course the main subject-matter is the Bible. But it is now possible to examine the various books more critically and to change slightly the point of view. In the Old Testament the various strands of which the historical books are woven can be explained, and the prophets put in their place of honour. The development of thought throughout the period can be roughly traced, and the gradual enlightenment of the Jews compared both with other ancient religions and with the full revelation given by and in Jesus Christ. In the New Testament too the emphasis shifts. Something can be learnt of the early church for which the gospels were written, and the simple story of love and sacrifice enriched by a fuller realisation of the mystery of which it is a part, the mystery of Incarnation, Redemption and Resurrection which is the text of every sermon of St. Peter or St. Paul.

Teaching at this stage will have two clear purposes. In the first place it must be objective. The Bible must be allowed to speak for itself, to give the message intended by the writer of the book studied for those for whom it was written; interpretation must never degenerate into distortion or suppression (on this point, as on the whole question of scripture teaching, the Spens Report can be consulted with profit). Incidentally, there seems to be no reason why this objective teaching should not be considered by the Board's Inspectors, at the same time and in the same way as any other subject. They may not be able to test sincerity or "willingness" but they can assess "competence".

But no teacher of intelligent adolescents will be able to teach the New Testament and to ignore theology; and if the attempt were made no self-respecting class would allow it to succeed. To St. Paul and his fellow-workers a distinction between the Christian faith and Christian conduct would have been not so much false as unintelligible. The life that they lived was what it was simply because of what they believed. "I have been crucified with Christ; yet I live; and yet no longer I, but Christ liveth in me: and that life which I now live in the flesh I live in faith, the faith which is in the Son of God, who loved me, and gave himself up for me." The man who wrote that would have had little patience with any form of Christian instruction which sought to ignore Christian doctrine.

But it is just here that we come across our main stumbling-block. The unhappy dissensions in the Church have produced the impression that to attempt to teach doctrine (which by its opponents is always called dogma) is to bring to life in the school the controversies which rage outside. No one I imagine will want to do that, at any rate at this stage; though the unhappy suggestion that ministers of various denominations should be admitted to the school to give instruction to their own particular flocks on their particular aspects of the faith would have just that effect.[1] But it is surely overlooked by most objectors that the fundamental truths of Christianity are universally accepted by all Christian sects; the difference comes elsewhere, in matters of additional beliefs, of exact interpretations, of methods of worship. It should not be beyond the power of a joint committee to draw up a simplified version of the creed which would obtain the universal acceptance of all Christian communions. The Nature and the Fatherhood of God, the Divinity of Christ, the Incarnation, the Crucifixion and Resurrection, the main outlines of the doctrine of Redemption, Eternal Life, in this rough summary we have those essential beliefs held by Christians throughout the centuries. And these are the things which matter. The ignorance of the normal child of 13 on such subjects must be experienced to be believed. At present this ignorance is rarely dispelled, with the result that the young people of our country grow up not really knowing what they believe nor why they believe it; such are readily blown over by the first breath of criticism, particularly if this is presented as a new view-point, a modern outlook which has triumphed over antique superstitions.

Of the post-certificate stage I need not speak at length, since it affects only a small though important minority. Clearly the emphasis shifts again, and there should be some attempt here to include some church history and more detailed study of such books as Isaiah, Job, the gospel of St. John and the major epistles. Discussion of points of doctrine and perhaps a consideration of some parts of "Doctrine in the Church of England" will be interesting and helpful, provided always that it is conducted by someone who can speak with a measure of authority; not to lay down the law but to check false assertions and settle points of difficulty.

This last point brings up again the question of the teacher. The Archbishops' letter laid down the two necessary qualifications of "competence" and "willingness", but it is not so easy to define these terms as it is to accept them. Clearly no one should be forced to teach the subject, and no one should be allowed to teach it who is manifestly unfitted to do so. But does the first proviso mean that no one should occupy a position which normally involves the teaching of scripture unless he or she is willing to teach it? We have already considered the question of Head teachers; but the difficulty may arise in filling ordinary staff vacancies. In the elementary school, where the personal touch is

---

[1] I hope that nothing I say will be construed as casting any reflection on the excellent work done in Church schools. I have not dealt with them separately in the essay, partly because the problems discussed for the most part do not concern them, and partly because I cannot believe that the dual system is more than a transitional phase.

of most importance and the knowledge required not excessive, it is probably best for the regular class teacher to take the Scripture lesson. It is true that if the time of the Scripture hour ceased (as the Archbishops suggest) to be the same for all classes this lesson could be delegated to another; and then no applicant would have to offer this subject, provided there were already enough Scripture teachers in the school to cover the ground. But where this is not the case then clearly willingness and capacity to teach this subject should be a condition of appointment. In secondary schools where the knowledge demanded is more extensive there is a growing demand for specialists in Scripture, to teach themselves in the higher forms and to guide the teaching throughout the school. The qualifications for advanced instruction here should be the same as in all other subjects; indeed they must be if the respect and interest of the pupils are to be retained. Unfortunately the supply is by no means equal to the demand, and is not likely to be for some years to come. A continuation of the revival of interest in the subject and the proposed change in its status in training colleges may in due course give us all the specialists we need. But till then we may have to stress willingness and not to inquire too closely into competence. Sincerity and enthusiasm will go far; and knowledge, unlike these qualities, can be acquired, even by the middle-aged. So that given the goodwill we should not do too badly.

And taking the schools as a whole the goodwill is there, ready to co-operate, to accept suggestions, to work out constructive programmes. In this subject, as in many others, the criticism which was at first levelled at our schools is becoming more and more focused on the "lost years" from 14 to 18, when the great majority of our young people are left without guidance or supervision. The contrast between the religious atmosphere of school and that of the factory and the street-corners being what it is, how *can* we hope that any but the most robust faith will survive? More important than the improvements which must be made in the schools are the measures we must devise for linking up schools with the world beyond. How far is this necessity present in the minds of those who are everywhere forming youth committees and selecting organisers for the "service of youth" movements in different parts of the country? There is here, surely, a magnificent opportunity for joint church action. Leaders of boys' and girls' clubs and other voluntary organisations, directors of education and individual members of the clergy could do great things if a strong lead were given. Somehow or other we must carry over the good work which is done at school into that indeterminate period when the results of it are at present lost for ever, unless the home atmosphere is such as to strengthen and deepen the religious life of its members. Is not this almost the first claim we ought to make upon the Churches? How many of them at present aim any of their energies at this particular age-group? They have their Sunday schools, which sometimes do little more than duplicate less efficiently the work of elementary teachers, and which in any case are unsuited to older pupils. And they have their Mattins and Evensong, appealing with greater or less success to congregations of adults. There are of course youth groups attached to a number of churches of all denominations, but even where these exist how far is any attempt made in them to give definite instruction and guidance in the application of Christian principles to everyday life?[1] If the teachers in elementary and senior schools could hand on their children with confidence to the clergy of the different denominations in their home parish, knowing that their spiritual education would be cared for and their problems considered with sympathy and understanding, then they would throw off their crippling sense of frustration and teach with a new hope.

So we come to the conclusion that the importance of religion in the school curriculum will depend much upon the general Christian atmosphere of the school; much upon the opportunities given for worship; much upon the scheme of teaching and the sincerity and skill of teachers; but most of all upon the steps that are taken to build on these foundations and ensure that they have not been laid in vain. It is to this great task that the Church is called to-day.

---

[1] Confirmation lies outside the scope of this essay. Clearly where children come forward for confirmation the situation is quite altered.

EQUALITY OF EDUCATIONAL OPPORTUNITY

Since Mr. Lyon's essay was written, the Trade Union Congress has demanded the abolition of the dual system of elementary education which is, incidentally discussed by the Rev. F. C. Pond in the essay that follows. The T.U.C. has also called for the surrender by the Church of even the partial control of any State-aided schools. The T.U.C. was not opposed to colourless "religious teaching", and it did not appear that the delegates objected to the agreed syllabuses that have been adopted in some areas. It has, however, to be recognised that organised labour has formally expressed its hostility to the objectives advocated by both Mr. Lyon and Mr. Pond.

It would be lamentable, at this time, if the Church and the Trade Unions were to be sharply opposed on the supremely important question of the nation's educational system, and there is evident danger that such opposition would be fully exploited by the forces of reaction. It will be difficult for the Church and the Roman communion, which is properly concerned for the preservation of the schools, for the foundation and upkeep of which its members have made great and persistent sacrifices, to come to a workable understanding with labour, but it should not be impossible. In any circumstances it is well that the Church's position should be made clear, and the recent developments have given these essays an increased interest.

Malvern urged that to make equality of opportunity a reality, there must obviously be a radical change in the whole system of national education. Such a change has been much discussed in the press and it is a matter of common knowledge that it is being considered by the Board of Education. The Church was the pioneer of elementary education in this country and there are in existence to-day over 9,000 Church Elementary Day Schools. It is therefore profoundly interested in the proposed educational reforms.

It should also be remembered that the majority of the Public Schools are Church Schools, that the Church has done much in the field of higher education during the past 100 years, including the creation of the Scotch Schools of the Woodard Foundation, and that there are many schools attached to Cathedral Churches.

The charge made in certain secularist circles that the Church is seeking to use the present crisis to control national education for its own ends is grotesquely untrue. But the Church does insist that no education can be regarded as satisfactory unless it is "inspired by a conviction of the supremacy of spiritual values".

The ideal and the method of a Christian education are explained in his essay by the Headmaster of Rugby, while the Rev. F. C. Pond, who was for some time an official of the National Society and is in close touch with the discussions that are now taking place, puts forward suggestions for attaining the Malvern objective of unqualified equality of opportunity.

EQUALITY OF EDUCATIONAL OPPORTUNITY

By THE REV. F. C. POND

"Every child should have the opportunity of an education till years of maturity, so planned as to allow for his peculiar aptitudes and make possible their full development. This education should be thoroughly inspired by faith in God and find its focus in worship." So writes the Archbishop of Canterbury in his Penguin special, *Christianity and the Social Order*. Dr. Temple is asking for equality of educational opportunity and such equality can only become a reality in this country when we have secured a national system of education. After this has been achieved it will then be possible for every boy or girl in the country, who possesses the necessary intellectual qualifications, to pass on from the primary to the secondary school and then to the university. It is true that to-day an increasing number of the sons of humble parents are entering the universities, but the road is often extremely difficult; the competition is severe and frequently the bursaries are not sufficient to enable these undergraduates to live in reasonable comfort.

The existing educational system of the country is of a complex nature and before proceeding further it may be wise to tabulate the main types of schools, and to explain the meaning of certain technical terms which must inevitably be used.

ELEMENTARY SCHOOLS

(*a*) The Provided Schools, i.e. Council Schools.

(*b*) The Non-Provided Schools, i.e. Church and other voluntary schools.

The above are sub-divided into:

Infant Schools or classes (up to 7 +).

Junior or Primary Schools (up to 11 +).

[N.B.—Many Junior Schools possess an Infants' Department.]

Senior Schools (sometimes called Central Schools) from 11 + to 14.

(*c*) Junior Technical Schools—for "selected" children between the ages of 11 + and 16.

Junior Technical Schools receive children from Primary Schools either as a result of examination or through the recommendation of a head teacher.

DAY SECONDARY SCHOOLS

(*a*) The Provided Day Secondary Schools, i.e. Council Secondary Schools.

(*b*) The Non-provided or Grant-aided Secondary Schools— the Grammar Schools, the City Company Schools and the like belong to this category. As the term "grant-aided" suggests, these schools receive financial assistance and in return reserve a proportion of their places for scholarship children, but the large majority attending these schools are "fee paying" pupils.

Note—The terms "Provided" and "Non-Provided" refer to the ownership of the bricks and mortar of the actual school building. Thus a Provided school means that the school building has been built or *provided* by the Local Education Authority. Conversely a non-provided school means that the school building was not built, i.e. *not provided* by the Local Education Authority but by some voluntary body.

Amongst the elementary schools there is the problem of the dual system caused by two different types of schools—Church and Council—the managers of Church Schools possessing the right of appointing their own teachers subject to a veto from the Local Education Authority on educational grounds. This system causes certain administrative difficulties.

During the last twenty years there has been a large growth throughout the country in the number of day secondary schools. This has been one of the most marked features of recent educational development, but here again there are two main types of schools—the council secondary and the older established schools. The latter, which used to be financially independent, have all had to receive assistance. They are called grant-aided secondary schools. In addition there are the large number of privately-owned preparatory schools, and finally the great public schools. How can these many different types of schools be welded together into one National System of Education? The solution is not an easy one because vested interests are involved, administrative problems must be solved, and finally further legislation would become necessary. The present position cannot be understood until it is realised that the State is a comparatively late-comer in the educational field. At the beginning of the last century the Church of this country was the great pioneer in elementary education. The British and Foreign School Society (a Nonconformist body) was founded in 1808, and the National Society for Promoting the Education of the Poor in the Principles of the Established Church, in 1811. These important religious organisations soon became the great educational champions of the poorer classes of the community.

Until 1833 these new voluntary schools, which had been established in large numbers throughout the country, were supported wholly by voluntary contributions and fees. In 1833 the Treasury for the first time, made a grant of £20,000 per annum for the erection of new schools, and this money was distributed on the recommendation of the two educational societies mentioned above. From 1839 onwards building grants were made by the newly appointed Education Department. But it was not until the passing of the Education Act of 1870—which made education compulsory for all children between the ages of 5 and 13[1]—that the State for the first time in our history subsidised the newly-appointed School Boards to help them in the building, equipping and maintaining of Board Schools. But by this time there were already in existence over 12,000 Church of England schools, in addition to Roman Catholic, Nonconformist, Jewish and other voluntary elementary schools.

When at last State elementary schools were founded, the policy was not to compete with existing schools but to supplement the efforts which had already been made. The State therefore never built a school in a locality where a Church school was already in existence. This explains why the majority of our village schools are Church schools and conversely why the majority of the schools in the big towns are Council schools.

Another point should be noted. The Church not only built schools but she also provided colleges for the training of teachers to staff those schools. Thus the Church was also the pioneer in the work of training teachers.

From 1870 to 1902 the State gradually took a larger share in the elementary education of the country. Then came the Education Act of 1902, and it is impossible to exaggerate the importance of this event, because with the placing of this Act upon the statute book of England the seed had been sown which was capable of producing a National System of Education. To the vast majority of the people, however, (particularly to Church folk) the main provision of the Act was that section which compelled the newly formed Local Education Authorities to maintain the non-provided schools. Hitherto these schools had received grants but under the provisions of the 1902 Act they were to receive far greater financial assistance.

Briefly the position of Church schools was that the School

[1] Compulsory attendance between these ages was merely a permissive by-law. In practice this was subject to numerous exemptions.

Managers now became financially responsible only for the land-lords' liabilities, whilst the Local Education Authority became responsible not only for the tenants' repairs but also for the upkeep of the school, i.e. teachers' salaries, all necessary books and equipment, lighting, heating and cleaning. Those conditions prevail to-day.

Valuable as those concessions were, the epoch-making provisions of the 1902 Act were to be found in Part II, which concerned itself with higher education. Section 2 (1) contained these words: "The L.E.A. shall consider the educational needs of their area and take such steps as seem to them desirable, after consultation with the Board of Education, to supply or aid the supply of education other than elementary, and to promote the general co-ordination of all forms of education. . . ."

The State, with very wide powers, at last entered the field of higher education, and the logical sequence of that step is the large number of magnificent Council secondary schools which have been built in recent years. In addition, scholarships and bursaries have been provided to enable boys and girls not only to pass from the elementary to secondary schools, but also to the university. All this was made possible by the passing of the 1902 Act. It is important to notice in passing that the provisions made for the giving of religious instruction in Council elementary and Council secondary schools are not the same. The former schools are governed by the Cowper Temple clause of the Act of 1870 which says that "no religious catechism or religious formulary which is distinctive of any particular denomination shall be taught in the school". The result of this clause is that the children attending these schools receive what is often described as "simple Bible teaching", but the Board of Education has ruled that the Apostles' Creed, the Lord's Prayer and the Ten Commandments are not "religious formularies distinctive of any particular denomination".

The negative provisions of the Cowper Temple clause apply only to Council elementary schools. They do not apply either to the Council secondary or grant-aided secondary schools. In both these latter types of schools denominational teaching may be given to the children of those parents who wish them to receive it. Such teaching is given on the school premises and during school hours.

Wherever denominational teaching in Council secondary schools is provided, it is usually given at the expense of the denomination to which the child belongs, i.e. the Church provides the teacher. On the other hand in the grant-aided secondary schools the school provides the teacher.

Another educational advance was made by the passing of the Education Act of 1918. The main heading of the first seven sections of the Act is: "National System of Education"—and Section I contains the following: "With a view to the establishment of a national system of public education available for all persons capable of profiting thereby, it shall be the duty of the council of every borough and county borough, so far as their powers extend, to contribute thereto by providing for the progressive development and comprehensive organisation of education in respect of their area . . . and shall when required by the Board of Education, submit to the Board schemes showing the mode in which their duties and powers under the Education Acts are to be performed and exercised. . . ."

The above refers only to those Authorities which are L.E.A.s both for Part II and Part III of the Education Act of 1902.[1]

Prior to the passing of the 1918 Act L.E.A.s were not compelled to have any scheme. In brief it can be stated that the Act of 1902 gave permissive powers to Part II and Part III Authorities. Some authorities used them whilst others did not. The 1918 Act made of obligation that which hitherto had been merely permissive.

Section 2 (1) (a) of the same Act provided that it should be the duty of the Local Education Authority responsible for elementary education "to make, or otherwise to secure, adequate and suitable provision by means of central schools, central or special classes, or otherwise

(1) for including in the curriculum of public elementary schools, at appropriate stages, practical instruction suitable to the ages, abilities and requirements of the children, and

(2) for organising in public elementary schools courses of advanced instruction for the older or more intelligent children in attendance at such schools, including children who stay at school beyond the age of 14." [2]

These and other provisions in the Act did a great deal indirectly to emphasise the need for a thorough re-organisation of the arrangements for the education of children below the age of 11. From 1919 much progress was made with the development of elementary education on the lines contemplated in the Act of 1918. Some L.E.A.s made provision for primary schools for children between the ages of 7 and 11 and with this development

---

[1] L.E.A.s having powers in respect of higher education are sometimes referred to as Part II Authorities—and L.E.A.s having powers in respect of elementary education only are referred to as Part III Authorities.

[2] The Education Act of 1918 raised the school-leaving age to 14 and allowed no exemptions.

there sprang up a certain number of senior or central schools for children between the ages of 11 and 14. In Circular 1350 (of 28 January, 1925), the Board of Education pointed out that the age of 11 was increasingly being recognised as "the most suitable dividing line between what may be called 'junior' and 'senior' education.

"The logical outcome of the whole trend of development was clearly shown in the Consultative Committee's *Report on the Education of the Adolescent, 1926*, which set out a general scheme for post-primary education for pupils from the age of 11+. The Report pointed out that primary education should be regarded as ending at about the age of 11+, and that a second stage should then begin, ending for many pupils at 16+, for some at the age of 18 or 19, but for the majority at the age of 14+ or 15+. The principal recommendations of this Report were accepted by the Board, and are now being carried out by L.E.A.s. Under the schemes of re-organisation drawn up by Education Authorities on the lines indicated in the 'Report on the Education of the Adolescent,' arrangements are being made for the provision of post-primary education for children above the age of 11, and in many instances the older children over the age of 11 have been taken from the former 'all age' schools to selective or non-selective modern schools."[1]

Rapid progress was made with the re-organisation of the elementary schools of the country, on the lines recommended in the Consultative Committee's *Report on the Education of the Adolescent, 1926*. In the big cities re-organisation presented less difficulties than in the country districts. In the former case it was a common practice to convert three 'all age' council elementary schools of a district into junior schools—with or without infant departments, and to convert a fourth school into a senior school for boys and girls over the age of 11+. These three junior (or primary) schools thus fed one senior or post-primary school.

In the country districts the position was more difficult because the senior schools in most cases had to be built. In theory, the small village "all age" elementary schools became junior schools and their children were transferred at the age of 11+ to the area senior school, which normally was situated in the nearest country town. This arrangement is open to serious criticism on the grounds that by transferring a country bred boy to a town school at the age of 11+, it is easy for such a child to regard the town as being superior to the country. In one case where all the "contributory" junior schools were situated in the country the

[1] "The Report of the Consultative Committee on the Primary School," p. 18.

new senior school, to which the children were transferred, was deliberately built in the country and not in the town.

The child, then, who begins his education in an elementary school commences in an infant school or department, and at the age of 7 + passes on to the primary school. On reaching the age of 11 he sits for the special place examination, upon the result of which far too much depends. A very few children, because of their success in this examination, are able to proceed to a secondary school proper. The number of such children, however, is really small, at least judging from my experience in East London, where if one of our children won such a scholarship the event was so rare as to justify the flying of flags and the granting of a holiday to the whole school. A certain number of children pass on to junior technical school, i.e. a school which is akin to the old higher grade school. The children are expected to remain until they reach the age of 16, and the education given might be described as ultra modern secondary, i.e. in addition to the normal subjects provision is made for commercial subjects. These schools often possess what is called a local bias. For example, a technical school situated in Portsmouth would probably assume that the vast majority of the boys would enter the dockyards on leaving school. The last two years of the school course therefore include such practical subjects as would be of future use to them in their work.

Whilst then a very small number of children to-day pass on at the age of 11 + from the junior to the secondary school proper and a much larger number to a technical school, the overwhelming majority of the children are transferred to the senior or modern school. Perhaps the main feature of these schools is the provision they make for handicraft and domestic subjects.

It will be seen, therefore, that to-day it is possible for a boy to begin his education in a small village elementary school, to pass from there by means of scholarship to a secondary school and eventually on to the university. Everything, however, depends upon the winning of scholarships and the competition is extremely severe.

In the meanwhile the managers of Church elementary day schools were able to hinder these progressive schemes for re-organisation. All too frequently they were unable to provide their own senior schools or departments because of financial difficulties, and unwilling to transfer their children when they reached the age of 11 + to a council senior school. Moreover, L.E.A.s were unable, legally, to transfer them. To meet this situation the Education Act of 1936 enabled L.E.A.s to give grants (under certain conditions) to the managers of Church schools of from 50 per cent to 75 per cent for the building of senior schools. The main condition for the receiving of a building grant concerned the appointment of teachers. It will be remembered that under the dual system of Church and Council elementary schools the managers of the former schools appoint their own teachers. This method of the appointment of teachers presents administrative difficulties to L.E.A.s. But it is obvious that if a Church school is to be a Church school in reality, and not merely in name, it is essential that the head teacher should believe and practice the faith which he teaches his children. It is also most desirable that the same should be true of the assistant teachers.

The 1936 Act recognised the truth of this position, but at the same time desired to evolve some method whereby, without doing a spiritual injustice to the Church schools, L.E.A.s should in future appoint the teachers to those senior schools which had received a grant. The solution was found in what were called "Reserved Teachers". A reserved teacher was appointed by the L.E.A., but before the appointment was made, the managers were allowed to satisfy themselves that the proposed teacher was fit and competent to give religious instruction. Only "Reserved Teachers" were to give denominational teaching. The proportion of reserved to non-reserved teachers on the staff of such a school was to be the subject of an agreement between the managers and the L.E.A. The then President of the Board of Education stated in Parliament, when the Bill was before the House, that if a Church school was to maintain its own special atmosphere it was obviously desirable that the head teacher should be a "Reserved Teacher". It is to be hoped that that section of the Act which allows L.E.A.s to give building grants will be revived after the war in the case of those Church schools whose schemes had reached a reasonably advanced stage before September 1939. The 1936 Act also raised the school-leaving age to 15, but unfortunately it allowed a loophole, and L.E.A.s were given powers to grant exemptions under certain conditions.

Reference has been made to the scholarship system whereby boys and girls may pass on from the secondary school to the university. Such State scholarships date from 1920. At first 200 scholarships were available for children from grant-aided secondary schools. In those days there were practically no Council secondary schools. In 1939 the number of scholarships had increased to 360 (tenable for 3 or 4 years), available both to those attending grant-aided or State schools. The number of State scholars at the universities at the outbreak of the present war was about 1,110. Grants came from the State, L.E.A.s, colleges, schools, and outside bodies.

The above facts will show how inadequate the provision was, and that there must have been a large number of boys and girls, who would have benefited by a university education, but were prevented by lack of funds. In addition the opportunities vary according to the district in which a boy or girl may live. This same disadvantage applies with equal force at other periods of the boy's educational life. Many country boys are at an educational disadvantage because they live in the country and not in a big city.

Another serious criticism of the existing scholarship arrangements is that its monetary value is often not sufficient to allow the student to enjoy a reasonably full life at the university. The result is that the student must obtain additional financial support from elsewhere, and if he is the son of poor parents his difficulties may become acute.

Boys and girls at a secondary school who express a desire to enter the teaching profession may go up to the university at the age of 18 for a four-year course, usually three years in arts or pure science and the fourth year in a teaching course. The considered opinion of an increasing number of people to-day is that the earmarking of scholarships for future teachers is undesirable. Two obvious criticisms come to mind. The first is that it is unfair to expect boys or girls to decide at the age of seventeen or eighteen that they wish to devote the whole of their lives to the teaching profession. The other criticism is that the system is liable to be abused, because it is possible for a boy to use this method of obtaining a university degree.

Before offering some criticisms of the existing system it may be well to remind readers that when a child reaches the ages of 11 + and leaves the primary school, three different types of post-primary or secondary education are available for him. In theory the child passes on to that particular type of secondary education which will best suit his needs. If he is the intellectual type he goes to the secondary school proper, whilst others pass on either to the modern or else to the technical school.

An illustration will help to reveal one weakness of the present system. Thomas Smith, the son of a poor man, having reached the age of 11 + leaves his primary school and passes on to the senior school. For him that is considered to be the best type of secondary education. On the other hand William Jones, who because he is the son of a doctor, goes to a day secondary school, because his father is able to pay the fees. He arrives at the age of 8. Intellectually Jones and Smith are very similar, but because

Jones's father can afford to pay the fees, he is still at the secondary
school from the years of 11 + onwards—the very school which
would be considered unsuitable for him if he was the son of a
poor man.

The poor boy therefore reaches the secondary school proper
only if the authorities consider that that particular type of education is suitable for him.   On the other hand the son of a more
wealthy parent may go to a secondary school proper merely
because his father can afford to pay the fees.

Further, the great public schools provide no free places and
they are closed to the boys of the primary schools.

FUTURE DEVELOPMENTS

What has been written above endeavours to outline briefly the
development of the educational system of the country from the
beginning of the 19th century to the outbreak of the present war.
An enormous amount has been achieved but still more must be
done if a national system of education is to become a reality.
The objective must be nothing less than equality of educational
opportunity for all.   How can this be attained?

Plans for future development must commence with the primary
school.   It is now agreed by most people that primary education
shall cease when the child reaches the age of 11 +, and that
at that age there shall be a complete break in the school life
of the child.   Moreover, it is important that he should then
leave that particular school building, and staff, and begin afresh
elsewhere.

A very considerable number of existing primary schools are
voluntary schools, and the vast majority of them belong to the
Church.   At once then the problem of the dual system arises.
The time has come when it must be tackled, but this does not
mean that it must be abolished. To my mind that would be
nothing less than a catastrophe.

It will be remembered that the powers of the L.E.A.s over
Church schools are limited.   The managers appoint the teachers
(subject to a veto by the L.E.A. on education grounds), and
whereas the L.E.A. controls the "secular"[1] instruction they
are not able to alter the organisation of a Church school, i.e.
they cannot convert an existing "all age" elementary school for
children between the ages of 5 and 14 into a junior or a senior
school.

A voluntary school which has thirty or more children on the
register cannot be closed even if there is a Council school next

[1] To the Christian no instruction is "secular".   This division of the subjects on the
time-table into secular and religious gives a false conception of life.

door which has empty classrooms. Such a school can only be closed if there is another school of the same denomination at hand, to which the children can be transferred. A new Church school may actually be opened in spite of the fact that there may be a Council school close by capable of housing all the children. The present method of the appointment of teachers to Church schools presents undoubtedly one of the greatest problems. L.E.A.s dislike it mainly on the grounds that it adds to administration difficulties. The teachers dislike it for the obvious reason that the Church possesses this power of private patronage. Headships, of which the Church has the disposal of some thousands, are coveted posts. Why, they ask, should one profession possess such powers over the members of another?

In addition to these administrative difficulties it is pointed out with truth that many existing Church day school buildings are old and often bad. The managers of these schools find it difficult to raise sufficient funds to keep even the existing buildings in a tolerable state of repair and utterly impossible to provide the funds for improvements and enlargements. In justice to the Church schools it is only fair to reply to those who criticise the existing buildings that that is the price which every pioneer has to pay. Church schools are of necessity old fashioned because they were first in the field. It is surely to the everlasting credit of the Church of this country that she cared so much for the welfare of the children of the poor that she had built 12,000 schools before the State built one. This enormous enterprise cost her millions of pounds, not only upon buildings but also upon their maintenance and the training of teachers. In any plans of reconstruction let us not forget how much we owe to the Church for all she has done in the past for the education of the poor man's son.

At this juncture a short digression on the subject of the value of the Church school to the nation may be helpful. The Church, because she is the Church, has a definite contribution to make in the sphere of education—a contribution which the State cannot make because the State *is* the State. The Church school—which is a Church school in fact and not merely one in name—is a monument erected in the country proclaiming what we as Christians mean by education. Education seeks to develop the whole child as made by God—body, mind and soul. It therefore desires to send the child into the world not only with a fit and healthy body and an alert and developed mind, but also with a healthy soul in touch with spiritual realities.

The Church school can satisfy the spiritual needs of the child by teaching him the faith of the Church of his baptism, by training him in worship and what is far more difficult but so important it is able to help the child to realise his membership within the fellowship of the Church.

The Church school consists of these three component parts— the parish school, the parish church and the parish priest. The latter should regard himself as the school chaplain and upon him rests the task of binding together the parish school and the parish church. The latter should be regarded and used as the school chapel. Under ideal conditions the Church school becomes the Church's nursery for the Church's children. The Church builds her schools not for her own sake—e.g. as a place where she can give her denominational teaching—but for the sake of God's children.

The real Church school, with its own delightful tone and atmosphere, can be a wonderful place. It has a contribution to make in the field of elementary education, and it would be a tragedy if those schools ceased to exist. In years to come we may have to face a decline in their numbers, but they must be allowed to make their special contribution.

The fact remains, however, that after the war many of these existing Church day schools must either be modernised or closed. It is greatly to be hoped that public opinion would not tolerate any large scale closure. Assistance from public funds, therefore, seems to be essential if they are to be saved, and this in turn will mean that L.E.A.s will expect to have a greater control over their management. The first and obvious demand will concern the method of the appointment of teachers, and I am prepared to believe that given good will on both sides an extension of the scheme of "Reserved Teachers" to those Church primary schools, which have received a building grant, is a workable scheme. In addition, L.E.A.s must be given powers to end the existing anomalies referred to above by the closing of redundant schools.

Primary education will cover the child's school life from the nursery school, through the infant school, and finally into junior school. It is to be hoped there will be a variety of such schools, and that entire State monopoly will be avoided. This can be secured if the voluntary schools are allowed to continue the work they have been doing during the last 130 years.

Elementary education (or the primary stage) ends at 11+. That which follows is therefore post-primary or secondary education. It is at this stage that one hopes to see big advances made. It has been previously stated there are in existence to-day three main types of post-primary schools:

(a) *The Senior School* for children up to 14. The 1936 Education Act raised the school-leaving age to 15, but exemptions were allowed.

(b) *The Junior Technical School* for children up to 16.

(c) *The Day Secondary School.*

(a) and (b) are administered as elementary schools and are thought of as such by the man in the street, but technically all schools for children over 11 + are secondary schools. It is essential therefore that in our future planning and thinking the modern (i.e. senior) and technical school shall receive the same treatment as the grammar school.

The experts are agreed that whilst the same type of primary education will suit the needs of all children up to the age of 11 they are of the opinion that differing types of secondary education are necessary. They consider that, in the main, three different kinds of secondary schools are needed, each offering a distinctive type of secondary education. Therefore, when the child attending an elementary junior school reaches the age of 11, in theory it passes on to that particular type of secondary school which will best be able to educate it. Some of these children may be sent to a grant-aided secondary school.

What is to be the future position of these important schools? Before they can be brought into a national system of education many problems must be solved. Their existence was based on the idea that in the main there must be two types of schools, one for the poor and another for the middle class. The labourer's son, therefore, went to the council school and the tradesman's son to the secondary school. The grant-aided secondary schools are self-contained units, possessing a junior school, and if a girls' school probably an infants' department. Because they provide an education in the same building for children between the ages of 8 and 18, they can be described as "all age" schools.

All the children attending them between the ages of 8 and 11 are there because their parents can afford to pay the fees. At 11 +, however, the conditions alter. These schools in return for the grants they receive from the L.E.A. must reserve a certain number of free places for scholarship children. A common percentage is 25 per cent and 75 per cent therefore of the pupils over the age of 11 are there because their parents can afford to pay the fees.

The important feature of these schools is that they provide an academic education. But a proportion of the 75 per cent fee-paying children are not capable of benefiting by this particular type of education, and provision has to be made for them accordingly. Therefore the grant-aided schools provide not merely the opportunities of an academic education but also the main characteristics which are to be found in the modern schools. It is true, of course, that these schools also give their children something which the modern school, as at present constituted, cannot give, viz. tone and prestige. The fact remains, however, that under existing conditions many children are to-day attending day secondary schools *not* because that particular type of education will best suit their needs, *but* because their parents can afford the fees.

In a National System of education the grant-aided secondary schools must become secondary schools in the technical sense of the word, namely post-primary schools, which shall concern themselves solely with post-primary, i.e. secondary education. Moreover, if we are to accept the opinion of the experts and accept the principle that one of the three types of secondary school shall offer an academic education, then the existing grant-aided secondary schools can satisfy this need. In brief it would appear that these grant-aided schools should confine their activities to post-primary education which should be of a purely academic nature.

Two consequences follow from this. The first is drastic. It means quite simply that all the children of the country shall begin their school lives in the primary school, and that all such schools shall be of the same status. There would be in the country the Church village school, with, of course, greatly improved and enlarged buildings. In the towns the Council junior schools and in the suburbs those private and preparatory schools whose buildings were capable of being made worthy. But the principle surely must be the same type of primary education for all.

One natural consequence of this drastic change would undoubtedly be the vast improvement of the junior schools of the country. There would not be a levelling down but a levelling up. To-day those who legislate are making arrangements for the education of the poor man's son, but as soon as they are legislating for the education of their own sons miracles would happen in the educational world.

The second inevitable consequence of the re-organisation of the grant-aided secondary schools will be the abolition of all secondary school fees. This is turn will mean that L.E.A.s must accept financial responsibility for these schools. This will raise certain problems to which I must refer later.

In the meanwhile one visualises all the children of the nation commencing their education in the same type of school—the primary or junior school. Whilst one advocates one type of school it is important to explain that this need not mean standardisation. Every scope should be given to head teachers to experiment and they should be encouraged to adapt their teaching to the particular needs of individual children.

At the age of 11 + primary education ceases, and the child then passes on to that particular type of secondary education for which he is best suited. Who is to make this all important decision and how is it to be made? The existing method is largely dependent upon whether a child is successful or not in a scholarship examination. Surely that method must cease and give place to one whereby the teachers and the parents in friendly council decide. Even so that decision must not be regarded as final. It is a well known fact that whilst some children develop intellectually later than others, yet others may be quick to learn whilst they are young and then fail to develop. Therefore, whilst a decision must be made when the child reaches the age of 11 +, the case should be reviewed again perhaps two years later so that if a mistake has been made it may be rectified. In this case the curriculum of all post-primary schools ought, as far as possible, to be similar for the first two years in order to facilitate this possible change of school at a later stage.

Under the above suggested schemes of re-organisation many interesting problems arise as soon as we begin to think of primary and post-primary education. It is important to keep before one's mind the fact that all types of schools which concern themselves with post-primary education, are in fact secondary schools. Hitherto one has thought of the Council senior school as being merely an elementary school for the older children of the poorer people. One must think of it as a secondary school which offers to its pupils its own specialised type of post-primary education.

If all schools for children over 11 are secondary schools it follows that they will all, in future, fall within the scope of higher education. Several interesting points arise because of this. The Cowper Temple clause (which forbids the giving of denominational teaching) only applies to Council elementary schools; therefore it will not apply to any of the secondary schools of the future. It is therefore to be hoped that use will be made of this opportunity, and that our senior boys and girls will be taught a more definite Christianity than is possible under the restrictive hand of Cowper Temple.

An interesting point arises as soon as Church senior schools enter the field of higher education. The present position of grant-aided secondary schools (which can be called voluntary or non-provided secondary schools) is that their management is under the control of a Board of Governors, on which the L.E.A. has a minority representation. The Governors appoint the teachers and are in control of the education which is given.

The L.E.A. has the power (but is under no compulsion) to assist these schools financially with regard to the repairs and even the enlargement of the building. Presumably if the L.E.A. is allowed to give one type of secondary school (the grant-aided) such assistance, it will be allowed to give another type of secondary school (the Church senior) the same assistance. It would appear logical to suggest that if the Church senior school is to enter the field of higher education it shall be treated in every respect as the existing grant-aided schools. One would therefore expect to see the Church senior school of the future under the management of a Board of Governors, appointing their own teachers and receiving financial assistance when necessary for the repairs, upkeep, and enlargement of the buildings.

In what has been written above only a slight reference has been made to the great public schools of the country, and a national system of education will not become a reality until they are brought into the system. If one pleads for "equality of educational opportunity suitable to the development of particular capacities", one must demand that the benefits which these great schools are capable of bestowing upon their pupils shall not be confined to the sons of those parents who are able to pay the fees. The present war-time method of the selection of officers for the armed forces of the crown may suggest a possible solution. To-day in our citizen army all men pass through the ranks, and a certain number of them select themselves for specialised training as future leaders. They pass on to O.C.T.U.s. Perhaps at some future date we may see the sons of the entire nation beginning their education in the primary school and some of these boys will eventually select themselves— on grounds of merit—for admission to the O.C.T.U.s of the educational world—the great public schools.

The above criticisms have suggested some of the weaknesses inherent in our existing educational system, but the strength of that system is largely due to the fact that there are varying types of schools. Educational experiments, sometimes of a daring character, have thus been made possible. This is good, and such experiments should be encouraged. This fact must be borne in mind when planning a national system of education. In order to attain that objective greater state control over all schools may become inevitable, but there is a grave danger that such control

may produce too great a standardisation. Whilst desiring to see
the many different existing types of voluntary schools welded
more closely together they must be encouraged to retain their
own individuality and traditions. Too much state control,
whilst giving to the country a magnificent national system
of education, might result in producing something which was
completely soulless.

MAN AND MONEY

The first five essays have dealt with various aspects of a Christian order of communal life. The Rev. W. G. Peck has, as his subject, the fundamental disease of the old order, that has inflicted on mankind such a tragic load of want and waste and war, and has meant frustration and suffering for the majority in every nation. We have rendered unto Mammon the things that are God's and we have paid a heavy penalty.

Malvern declared: "A system in which there is a distinct money interest, apart from the interest of the producers or of the community as a whole, tends to fall under the condemnation of usury. . . . The essential purpose must be to secure that money becomes a genuine register of economic fact, and, so far as it is also a force affecting that fact, is directed by consideration for the public welfare alone. Money should become functional to man in his economic activity, and the grounds of any suspicion that economic activity has become functional to money should be removed."

This contention is developed by Mr. Peck in his careful survey, one of his important conclusions being that industry has become "the servant of money", and that "judged by the criterion of human welfare in relation to world resources the monetary system is a fantastic distortion of reality".

MAN AND MONEY

By The Rev. William G. Peck

THE defence of the claim that there is, or at least may be, a Christian sociology, rests upon a three-fold assertion. In the first place, it is held that if sociology is to be more than a merely descriptive science, and is to pass to an understanding of the causes of social growth and decay, it must possess some criterion of social health. In the second place, it is declared that such a criterion cannot reside in pragmatic estimates of material achievements, since great material achievements have frequently carried within them the seeds of their own decline: that the necessary criterion must be concerned with some estimate of the nature of man, of what constitutes human well-being. And finally it is claimed that the Christian doctrine of man has at least a *prima facie* right to provide the foundation of the sociological criterion. Thus the Christian sociologist examines any given social order, any political structure or economic system, asking whether it is consonant with the ordained nature of man as that is conceived by Christian theology: whether it is, within its own scope, serving the attainment of that final purpose for which man is created and to which his nature is addressed.

The Christian doctrine of man involves a conception of human well-being. This is believed to depend primarily upon acceptance of the true end, the ultimate satisfaction, of human nature, which is God. But since, by reason of his situation in the physical world, man finds himself with a complex of needs requiring for their satisfaaction an approach to that physical world, the acceptance of God as his final satisfaction is somehow related to the satisfaction of his subsidiary needs. For his human personality, though engaged upon various levels, is a unity, and is affected in its wholeness by whatever affects it upon any plane of its activity. His whole nature, physical, psychological and spiritual, is organically one. His whole nature is concerned with what concerns any part of it; and therefore not only are his physical and psychological relations with the world controlled by the fact that he is a creature destined for an order beyond nature, but his approach to his spiritual end is conditioned by his place within nature.

The last consideration is of the utmost importance for our present study; for it is at once apparent that much depends upon a true judgement concerning man's relation with his natural environment, and upon the nature and extent of the satisfactions which he is entitled and able to derive from it. And this judgment, again, will be concerned with the question of positive human ability to realise and administer the resources of the physical world, and with the problem of how far success in such action can be brought into alignment with man's spiritual end and made to minister to his whole nature. That, indeed, is a problem which man, as spirit, is required to solve. Consequently, any minimising falsification of the facts concerning his power to control natural resources for the satisfaction of his physical need, is an interference with his specific spiritual task. It prevents the accurate statement of a problem, the solution of which is essential to man's own interior being; and it therefore cripples and confines the human soul and the human society.

It does more. It suggests an irrational opposition between the human powers of which man himself is aware, and the extent of the natural satisfactions which those powers are actually able to procure in the world. It comes to appear that man is somehow a misfit in nature. Nor is this conclusion escaped when it is made to seem that while human powers are capable of securing from the resources of nature a more abundant response to human need, the social organisation of economic effort cannot possible distribute the ensuing satisfactions beyond a certain rigidly defined limit, and that any attempt to do so must result in economic and social confusion. This assumption implies that the skill and energy of men, exercised beyond a certain point, are necessarily wasted, though the point where this begins to occur is well below what is required for human satisfaction. Again the suspicion arises that man in this world is a creature doomed to frustration. He cannot realise his own potentiality in relation to the potentiality of the natural world; and in that situation he can neither state nor solve problems which are native to him as "a cosmic spiritual being."

There is a yet further consideration. The falsification of the facts concerning man's relation to nature must condemn his social structure to unreality. And those who attempt to improve the structure only in accordance with ethical perceptions will themselves be impelled to false solutions. Thus, for example, the attempt to secure economic security within a situation of apparent economic scarcity, an attempt ethically irreproachable, may be forced to admit such sacrifices of personal liberty as will again lead to the conviction that there is an irremediable contradiction in man as he confronts the task of living in the world: that in this world he cannot be himself. The world is at the present time rich in social theories whose supporters have failed to consider

how the problem of social order would be affected if it were shown
that their proposals were proceeding upon a falsified account of
the human situation.

It is a thesis receiving constantly accumulating proof and
growing support, that the whole sociological situation of modern
man has been subjected to such a falsification as has produced the
results we have adumbrated. If this is true, it is a consideration
of the most profound and far-reaching import. There can be no
true estimate of the possibilities of man's life, there can be no
satisfying social design, there can be no valid conception of world
order, until that falsification is dismissed, and we proceed to live
upon a basis of reality. Only then shall we know what man can
do with his world. The thesis with which we are concerned is
that the modern monetary system has perpetrated such a falsification of man's relation with his world as has befogged and misdirected the whole modern enterprise.

A hundred years ago the thoughts and the lives of men were
dominated in a remarkable manner by the doctrine of relative
scarcity as a permanent economic factor. Malthus had declared
that population always tends to overtake the means of subsistence.
Ricardo had announced "the iron law of wages", and had implied
that there was no hope of any considerable improvement in the
material conditions of the masses of mankind. It is instructive
to observe that Lassalle's collectivist doctrine was shaped by
Ricardo's conclusions. Lassalle believed that there was no
alternative between the *dicta* of the early economics and state-
collectivism, and he supposed that collectivism alone could solve
the problem of production.

For those who, like Charles Dickens, while revolted by the
squalid poverty around them yet suspected that freedom must
disappear in a collectivist state, the dilemma was serious. We
may believe that the "benevolence" preached by Dickens, though
comparatively ineffective as an economic solution, was genuine
in intention; but to others it was acceptable on prudential
grounds. For social conditions, which the economists seemed to
regard as unfortunately necessary, appeared to threaten catastrophe: the two menaces of revolution and cholera. The growth
of "charity" as a social phenomenon of the period demonstrates
how widely men accepted the hypothesis of scarcity, and how
deeply they dreaded its social effects. In 1862, of the 640
charitable institutions existing in London, 279 had been founded
between 1800 and 1850, and 144 between 1850 and 1860.[1] It
was a sign that the Industrial Revolution which promised

[1] Humphry House, *The Dickens World*, p. 77.

wealth for some, threatened also social dissolution; and this
apparently meant that within the supposed limits of the wealth
that could be produced there must arise a social conflict, unless
some voluntary redistribution were undertaken to relieve the
worst features of the situation. There was not enough to go
round—there never would be enough to go round—to ensure
human decency for all. If this entailed the menace of social
revolt and eventual chaos, it was but another proof of the tragedy
of man's mysterious lot in this world.

Yet the modern economic system was not destroyed by a failure
to overcome a natural scarcity. It finally came to grief, and
involved mankind in a vast tribulation, because it failed to
eradicate its own interior self-contradictions. And the chief force
operating against every attempt to secure human justice within
the system, was that subordination of the economic operation to
the unbased, independent monetary rights for which the system
itself has provided a peculiar opportunity. To the claim that the
problem of production has been solved in our time, it must be
remarked that this solution has, quite unnecessarily, been made
to involve the acquisitive ravaging of natural resources, so that
we may yet have a world full of gadgets and short of food. But
that situation would be the result of the misuse of modern power-
techniques: it is not implicit in them.

The claim that production up to the level of a material basis
of the "good life" for mankind is within our power may, on the
whole, be admitted. And it may be remarked that no state-
collectivism has been necessary to produce this result. If Ricardo
and the early economics were wrong, so was Lassalle. There
was no truth in the supposition that the world's resources must
remain inadequate to human need. There was no truth in the
argument that only by placing the whole economic enterprise in
the hands of the political executive could the actual resources
be realised. The system did produce, and turned scarcity into
something like abundance. It was this achievement which
proved its undoing.

The modern economic has failed because, while it has been
able to realise the potential resources of the world, it could not
guarantee that this wealth would be effectively addressed to the
satisfaction of man. The ultimate source of this failure lies in
the dissociation of the various fields of human culture under
modern secularism. The economic enterprise, no longer addressed to the wholeness of man's being, has therefore dealt
with man, not as a spiritual being with an eternal destiny, but
merely as a factor in an economic process. The medieval
doctors had regarded economic action as intended to serve man's

whole nature, and its natural end was therefore to be found only in human satisfaction. It was this conception which lay beneath St. Antonino's reiterated assertion, "production is on account of consumption." And even if, from another point of view, consumption is on account of production, for the exercise of human powers in craftsmanship, artistic creation, and the works of the spirit, it remains true that it is man himself who supplies the whole economic process with meaning.

But the isolation of economic action from that wholeness of man's being which Christian philosophy had posited, and the reduction of man in his economic action to the position of an instrument, left the nature of the economic purpose undefined. The modern world, onward from the post-renaissance period, supplied the definition. The economic end, the regulative principle of work and trade, became money, a liquid profit, in a sense never accepted by medieval theology. To this end, no doubt, the satisfaction of human need might contribute. Man as consumer was a necessary factor of the money-seeking mechanism. But as the new system developed and money became not only the desired result, but the operative cause and initiator of work and trade, it was discovered that human deprivation might well, on occasions, help to preserve financial "stability", and secure that liquid profit which was now the only admitted reason for any economic action taking place in the world.

The system of the modern world was shaped by the accepted purpose. As production for money increased, it became increasingly necessary to limit the distribution of the product in the area of its production: to create an "unpurchasable surplus". It is to be observed that an unpurchasable surplus is one which cannot be exchanged for an equivalent import of desired goods; since, if the imported goods are to be distributed, there must be in people's pockets sufficient money to have bought the whole original production. The unpurchasable surplus must therefore be sent out of the area of production into other markets, there to capture purchasing power not distributed in wages and salaries in the course of its production. Thus commodity prices are kept up at home, and liquid profit is secured from foreign trade: a process which is of course defeated if imports are allowed to exceed exports. The coming of the power-machine, without any appreciable rise in wages or reduction of hours, procured, of course, a larger unpurchasable surplus; but it appeared at first to threaten large-scale unemployment and moved the workers to violent opposition. Yet throughout the nineteenth century, larger numbers of people were employed on the machines, because the growing "surplus" was disposed of in an expanding world market.

For such expansion the whole industrial system was shaped. When Hitler said that Germany must "export or die", he was speaking inaccurately, for it was never true that Germany or any other nation could live only in this way. But it is true that the system of financial industrialism places nations in the position that they must export or die—or renounce the system, as Germany eventually did. Yet it is precisely the growing impossibility of expansive export that has sounded the death-knell of the system and has brought to disaster the nations that have identified themselves with it. For since the liquid profit must tend to be invested in the further expansion of the productive process, the productive process by the machine has itself spread all over the world. Not only is this true, but the machine has advanced in speed and adaptability; and now we are said to be moving out of the machine age into an age of power technique. And it is alleged that whereas the machine at the height of its efficiency increased a man's productive power three hundred times, power-technique may increase his productive power three thousand times.

We must remember that this enormous potential world production has been operated by a system seeking to make a part of the product unpurchasable somewhere, in order that somewhere else it may secure a clear monetary gain. Since practically the whole world has come to share in this attempt, it is obvious that the "somewhere else" has become increasingly limited in area. The world market declines. "Expansion" becomes less and less possible. And the result is a world-surplus of goods, causing world-unemployment, which enforces a further decline in consumption and further unemployment. Thus, in face of an unprecedented potentiality of real wealth, there are poverty, hunger, and insecurity. Two factors had tended to relieve the situation before 1939. One was the virtual retirement of Germany from the world market. The other was the gradual increase of employment upon armaments. The peace-surplus could not be distributed. But it could be transformed into a huge accumulation of munitions: and thus was discovered the irrational market by which alone the system could be kept going.

Faced with the threatened collapse of industry, industrialists as well as workers have been eager to learn how the system may be refashioned so as to become a valid instrument of human purpose. The problem, stated in its technical term, is that of *price*—how to arrive at a price level which will make possible the consumption of the world's total product, and will therefore employ all the human energy and skill necessary to achieve that product. For if prices are too low, the producer cannot recover his costs, however great his sales may be. If they are too high, again he cannot recover his costs because his sales diminish. And although it is true that a rise in wages enables goods to be bought if there is no rise in their price, the fact is that rising wages are part of a rising price level. Usually a rise of retail prices precedes a rise of wages, and the wage increase merely restores the previous situation. The workers suffer because the producer is condemned to walk a tight rope between profit and loss. Prices will not securely cover costs and leave a margin. Why? What is the intractable element in "cost" which presents the hard core of resistance? Why cannot a high relative wage ensure the consumption of all goods in the shops, and still leave a working margin for the producer? Why must it force up retail prices, and thus leave goods still unpurchasable? This inability of men to buy and sell is the cause of unemployment. Then why could not a great undertaking of public works ensure the absorption of the unemployed without thereby, through the necessary taxation or loan-interest involved, causing a decreased public purchasing power which would only create further unemployment elsewhere?

It may be argued that the embarrassment of the producer is due to the fact that far too large a proportion of the "price" obtained for goods produced is absorbed in the payment of dividends to shareholders. But vast numbers of shareholders have received next to nothing from their investments during the years of our economic tribulation. Many have seen their capital disappear. And it is extremely difficult to believe that interest on investments has actually absorbed and redirected all the purchasing power which would have been required to distribute a determinative proportion of the world's unpurchasable surplus.

The whole practice and ethos of modern investment need careful examination in the light of Christian doctrine. That doctrine has been understood in recent days as implying that it is wrong to draw profits from business undertakings which underpay their employees or produce shoddy, useless or actually harmful commodities. But it has had a traditional implication which is even more germane to our present discussion. The medieval rules in restraint of usury implied that it was wrong to receive monetary profits from an enterprise in which the investor had not the slightest personal interest, except that of financial gain. Thus the business may pay its workers relatively well: it may produce excellent goods; but if the investor regards it as merely the means of monetary profit for himself, his investment is ethically at fault. And unquestionably a vast amount of modern

investment falls under judgement. Moreover, it is generally compelled to be investment in a production which is not "on account
of consumption".

But again, we have to consider that the transition from investment as a mode of personal interest in a corporate venture, to
investment as an impersonal mode of financial gain, is a phenomenon which has increased as industry has come to depend for
its ultimate financial basis upon the creation of bank credit.
Why this has been so we may be able to see at a later stage of our
argument. The main consideration which confronts us in our
search for the central cause of our economic embarrassment is
that behind all "investment" lie certain facts. That the most
consistently gainful enterprise in the modern world is not industry,
but finance. That the method of creating credit places a tax
upon real wealth. That bank credit is the governing factor in
production and consumption, and that its vast claim upon
industry and agriculture is the rigid, intractable element which
makes quite impossible the salvation of industry by industry
itself.

The whole discussion becomes completely unrealistic unless it
is understood that industry, conceived as a self-governing, independent entity, capable of shaping its own policies upon a basis of
reality, can no longer be said to exist. Industry is no longer its
own master. It is the servant of Money, which has now become
something more than the "end" of the economic process. Money
has become a power controlling the economic process for its own
ends. What was called "capitalism" has shown an affinity for
a monetary system which has raised all the vices and contradic-
tions of capitalism to a higher power, in the economic structure
now more properly termed financial industrialism. But the
problems of industry itself can no longer be reached and understood, except through an understanding and estimate of its
financial government.

The development of monetary technique is historically associated with commercial and industrial expansion, and reflects the
purpose of so treating the production and interchange of goods
and services as to produce a monetary profit, independently of
the consideration that "production is on account of consumption". The banking enterprise progressed, with the new economic
of loans for production, in the transition from the Middle Ages.
A series of monetary devices came into operation, increasingly
designed to provide, for the expansion of economic transactions,
an increase of money which would nevertheless leave the most
assured profit in the hands of the money-dealers. The discovery

that depositors were most unlikely all to desire the withdrawal of their deposits of coin at the same time, made it possible to lend a proportion of their deposits to borrowers. The banker had guaranteed that the depositor would receive his deposit on demand or at due notice; but it was found possible to re-lend a large part of the total deposits at interest which accrued to the banker and not to the depositor. This increased the velocity of the circulation of money, and thus assisted the expansion of commerce; but upon that expansion the banker laid his toll.

The further discovery that it was unnecessary to lend coin, and that paper promises to pay in metallic currency would circulate freely so long as "confidence" remained, made possible further extensions of credit-creation. The bankers issued their own notes; but in the period of experiment disasters occurred. Not seldom the note-issue was out of reasonable proportion to the currency held by the banks, and their inability to meet heavy presentations of notes for payment in coin caused panic and catastrophe. Eventually the issue of notes by private banks became illegal. But this only led to the third and final stage of development: the creation of bank-credit by book-entry, with the cheque system as its means of circulation.

Upon credit so expanded, the banks of course charged interest. Into the nature of this technique we are about to inquire; but at this point it must be remarked that the system to which we have become accustomed accumulates for the credit-creator a profit which depends upon the public acceptance of two assumptions: That money, since in the form of coin it is a commodity, is in itself a thing of value, and that a charge may justly be made for the loan of it. The actual metal presumably has an owner who exchanged for it some goods or services. The coin cost somebody something to produce—though in fact the coins lent by the first bankers were never produced, and more often than not were not owned, by those bankers. The second assumption underlying the banking system in its final stage is that an expansion of credit far beyond its actual physical basis in gold, may also be justly treated as a commodity, with an intrinsic value in itself, costing something to produce, and belonging to an owner who has a private right to decide its disposal. Whatever may be thought of the first assumption, the second is merely nonsensical.

The method of credit creation as it has become established in the modern world is now becoming widely understood; but there are still great numbers of intelligent people to whom the main facts are unknown, and it is therefore necessary briefly to state them, (although with the explanation that the necessities of war have modified the technique in some respects). The theory has

been that the gold-holdings of the Bank of England must determine the volume of the currency in circulation, save for what is
called "the fiduciary issue", which is a variable amount of
currency based upon the authority of the State. When currency
comes into the hands of the Joint Stock Banks, they regard it as
the basis from which to measure the amount of credit they may
"create", and if circumstances are favourable, they will issue
credit in the forms of loans and overdrafts to "credit-worthy"
customers, up to ten times the value of their currency holdings.
Upon this, they charge interest. And when the loan or overdraft
is repaid they will cancel and so destroy that amount of credit.
The money of our modern transaction is, to an overwhelming
extent, of this nature.

The Encyclopaedia Britannica (14th edition) thus explains the
operation: "Banks create credit. It is a mistake to suppose that
bank credit is created to any important extent by the payment
of money into the banks. A loan made by a bank is a clear
addition to the amount of money in the community." And there
is a great consensus of witness upon the main point. Mr. R. G.
Hawtrey declares bluntly, "When a bank lends, it creates money
out of nothing." Governor Eccles, President of the Federal Bank
of the United States, explains, "The banks can create and destroy
money. Bank credit is money. It is the money we do most of
our business with." Mr. J. M. Keynes says, "There can be no
doubt that all deposits are created by the banks." Mr. McKenna,
over and over again, declared that every bank loan is a deposit,
and that the banks create and destroy money. That money, we
must remember, is created by a stroke of the pen, and its cost to
the bank is practically negligible. Indeed, the whole method is
true to the principle enunciated by William Paterson when he
founded the Bank of England in 1694, "the bank to have the right
of interest of all moneys created out of nothing."

We have already implied that the lending of credit, thus
created, into circulation, for gain, is based upon an intellectual
confusion. Credit, in the sense of public monetary supply, ought
to be the implementation of a certain mathematical relationship.
When the creation of money disturbs that relationship, the result
is a misrepresentation of fact. The money of modern transaction,
being of the nature of credit, ought manifestly to be scientifically
related to the volume of goods and services with which it has to
deal. If it is regarded as possessing an intrinsic value in itself,
it becomes part of the public volume of goods, with a price
attached to it which, as it varies, must affect the power of men to
exchange all other goods.

Moreover, if credit-money is a commodity, its destruction presents a problem. Upon what ground can wealth be destroyed? We know that in commerce goods are destroyed in the hope of keeping up their price. But actually, the destruction of credit may result in an insufficiency of purchasing power to exchange a rising volume of goods. Thus what is to the advantage of the credit-creator is socially disadvantageous. The point we are concerned to make just here, however, is that the cancellation of credit to the disadvantage of the community proves that the banks do not finally regard it as wealth in itself, but as an instrument of gain. That is an intellectual inversion unworthy of acceptance by a rational society.

We have no quarrel with the practice of expanding and contracting the amount of money in a country. Obviously the amount of money must bear relation to the work it has to do. More goods will generally require more money. Less goods will need less money. But a guarantee is required that the issue of credit shall be adjusted, in the interests of the whole community, to these realities; and that guarantee the modern monetary system is unable to provide. We may quote the very plain words of Sir Reginald Rowe:

(1) It is indefensible that concerns trading for private profit should be allowed to create, out of nothing, and lend at interest, claims to other people's goods, or, alternately, to remove from circulation claims to goods which have already been produced.

(2) The policy which bankers decide to pursue is in the circumstances bound to be determined in the first place by what is likely to yield the concerns they serve the highest financial return, which is seldom the policy most advantageous to trade and industry, or most largely conducive to the common good.[1]

To the observation that, after all, the banks' profits are relatively moderate, considering their huge turnover, it may be replied that it is the nature of their right to this turnover that should be considered, and the fact that it seems capable of being so treated as to ensure the profits of the banks, no matter what happens to the profits of industry, the wages of the workers, and the price of a pair of boots or a pound of bacon. The size of the bankers' profits may be a matter for discussion. Their regularity through a period of general economic uncertainly is a further subject for inquiry. But the main question is whether there is any justification for a private business procuring a monetary profit, through the power to determine the volume of the public means of exchange, the true basis of which is the real wealth produced by the community. And the question becomes more

[1] *The Root of all Evil*, p. 10.

pointed when it is perceived that over a tragic period the manipu-
lation of credit has disabled the community from consuming a
large proportion of its own wealth. The decisions of the banks
as to the volume of credit to be issued, and the price to be charged
for it, have had this result. This is that falsification, of which we
have spoken, which frustrates the spirit of man. For we have
seen an enormous increase in the production of goods and services
turned into a human disaster, because the volume of credit, the
amount of purchasing power, has been inadequate to the task of
distribution. And its inadequacy has been engineered on behalf
of financial "stability".

The affinity between "capitalism" and banking lay in their
common interest in "expansion". For the banks, however, the
chief concern was the increase of fixed capital which this neces-
sitated, which might become the security for further profitable
credit creations. Credit, therefore, was for production: though
it was issued on terms which tended to place the producer in
difficulties, since it falsely increased his costs. But with the
advance of machine production throughout the world, and with
the appearance of power-technique which greatly increased the
ratio of production to the human labour employed, the problem
of selling the commodities became acute. An issue of credit
related to the necessity of consumption rather than to the
securities provided by fixed capital, would threaten the
"stability" of the credit system; and perhaps the most important
result of the situation was that industry passed increasingly
beneath the control of the banks, until "capitalism" became a
misnomer. Industry had become an instrument of money, and
the world learned to its sorrow that only that which was financially
possible and desirable was materially possible. The unpurchasable wheat, the meat, the coffee, the furniture, the clothing,
which were produced in abundance, could not be bought. They
seemed real enough, but lacking the life-giving substance of
money, they were mere appearances. Because they existed, men
were unemployed. Because they were financially "impossible",
men struggled in poverty.

The effects upon economic life of a distributing medium unrelated to what is to be distributed, but determining the amount
of the distribution, are widespread. Every season of prosperity
has to be paid for by some subsequent adversity, and the banks
struggle with the trade-cycle, which their own methods help to
create, by devices which are more of the nature of sympathetic
magic than of science. The investor becomes less and less a
participator in a joint human enterprise, and more and more
concerned with the purely financial results of industry. The

industrialist finds himself controlled by price-competition. He is compelled to battle, by means of the blarney of stimulative advertisement and high-power salesmanship, with all other producers, for sales; and with his workers, to resist wage-demands. Meanwhile both he and his workers, who are concerned with the real work, fall under the control of the financier who is concerned only with money. The workers themselves are trapped in the relation between wages and retail prices, and baffled by the fact that their work tends to produce a surplus of goods which cannot be sold, and thus itself to rob them of employment. The consumer, if his income is fixed, benefits by falling prices; but this is a situation which has to be "corrected" in the interests of financial stability. And if he has achieved, by combination, the power to demand wage-increases, the increase always lags behind the rise of retail prices. Thus the restriction of consuming power, in the interests of finance, is translated into human suffering and the degradation of human relations.

Meanwhile, the same financial operation extended upon a world-scale, has constantly intensified the process of turning world trade, as the interchange of mutually needed goods, into a fierce struggle to sell an identical product in a world-market in which there is an inadequate power to purchase it. There is an international scramble to capture purchasing power from foreign areas. World trade has ceased to be a genuine exchange. It has become a financial adventure in which the success of one nation is achieved at the expense of others. But the fact is that the attempt to extract a monetary return on credit from this world adventure is finally proving to be an attempt to reach the rainbow. All that the "successful" nation appears to achieve in the long run is a claim upon other nations for quite unpayable debts. The pre-war world was crowded with irrecoverable "favourable balances".

Thus, judged by the criterion of human welfare in relation to world resources, the monetary system is a fantastic distortion of reality. And the question to be decided, before any decision is taken concerning the rebuilding of our social and industrial structure, is whether money is to be accepted as determining the situation upon which those changes must proceed. If only what is financially possible is materially possible, it must be that the claims of human security, under the pressure of economic stringency, will tend to outweigh the claims of human liberty. If, however, as the President of the Bank of Canada has admitted, "whatever is materially possible and desirable is financially possible," the production which our present system forbids because it could not be distributed, would become available for the "have

nots". Monetary reform obviates the attempt to distribute a
falsely limited production; and it destroys the fear which makes
men willing to sacrifice freedom for a guaranteed subsistence.

The central issue is clear. If it is true that the system of
financial industrialism has come to confusion because of its
inability to distribute its production; and if that inability is
chiefly due to the control of manufacture, agriculture and trade
by a monetary system addressed to its own ends, it seems that the
restoration of a true relation between society and economic
reality can be accomplished only by a monetary system related
to the actual volume of goods and services available for distribution, and devised to place adequate purchasing power in the
hands of the community. And it goes without saying that money
must therefore be regarded as a costless, mathematically accurate,
indication of the real wealth involved, and must, indeed, distribute that wealth without adding to it a false element of cost
which, by destroying the Just Price, would prevent its total
distribution.

Total distribution of total production will ensure that all the
human labour necessary for the satisfaction of the needs of the
community will come into employment. And thus one of the
two end-products of financial industrialism—unemployment—
will be eliminated; and the human energy which, under power-
technique, is not required in economic production must be
trained to find its proper expression in creative leisure. Moreover, a monetary system which made possible total home-pur-
chase of the community's production would eliminate the
"unpurchasable surplus" by which it is attempted to extract a
"favourable balance" from foreign exchange. The home community, indeed, would not need to purchase its own total product; but it would be in a position to purchase an import of goods
equivalent to its own exported surplus. International trade
would then become an exchange of mutually needed commodities, goods for goods, and not an attempt of nations to pick
one another's pockets. This would go far to minimise the
occasions of war, which is the second end-product of financial
industrialism.

It will be obvious that this points to a more balanced internal
economy in England. This, indeed, is very likely to become
desperately necessary, as the world production of manufactured
goods makes it less possible for England to remain "the workshop of the world", and as the depredations of finance in the
world's primary-production areas, with the destruction of the

soil and the consequent menace of famine, make it more difficult
to secure food for our people. We shall need a great agricultural
revival, and an exchange of the products of field and factory
within our own borders. And we shall need a monetary instrument devised to ensure that the total product shall be exchanged
up to the level of our real needs, the surplus being devoted to
procuring from abroad a genuine equivalent of goods we ourselves
cannot produce.

To see in broad outline the nature of the monetary transforma-
tion required is not difficult. The community's natural ownership of credit must be recognised. The creation of credit by means
which inject a false element of cost into all economic transactions
must cease. Nor is there much difficulty in deciding how the
community's ownership of credit is to be implemented in the
creation of purchasing power. The policy of nationalising the
banks is, of course, almost meaningless unless it is accompanied
by a real understanding of the social effects of monetary technique.
Nor can any nationalisation which may place the power to
create or withhold public credit in the hands of a political party
temporarily in power, be regarded without alarm. What is
needed is a credit corporation established upon a charter which
will clearly define its public function and give it independence
of political influence. But the charter must make it clear that
money is a public mechanism for disseminating wealth.[1]

Greater problems arise, however, when consideration is turned
to the question of the principles upon which the distribution of
credit shall be conducted. It is well known that there are two
main schools of thought upon this subject. Those who argue for
Producer Credit as the best method, believe that it will be possible
thus to squeeze through the work-and-wages system a far greater
volume of purchasing power relative to retail prices of goods,
than can at present be achieved; and that at the same time this
will make some of our present social services unnecessary, while
allowing of considerable increases in others, e.g., pensions at an
earlier "old age", and possibly of family allowances. But we must
observe that if these latter distributions of purchasing power
are creations of new money, and not secured by taxation which
only moves already existing purchasing power, they are forms
of "consumer credit".

The more drastic school of thought accepts a thorough-going
consumer credit as the more satisfying method. It doubts
whether, with the advance of power-technique, the work-and-

---

[1] It goes without saying that the greater efficiency of service would be obtained by
the employment of the *personnel* of our present banking industry in the Credit Corporation. Their status would be "professional", and not "commercial".

wages system can remain as the general method of distributing purchasing power; and it therefore desires to have credit placed directly in the hands of all consumers. This inalienable income would be in addition to any sum earned by work. It seems that there is no rigid line of demarcation between the two schools, as far as their main purposes are concerned. The Producer Credit school has no objection in principle to the direct distribution of some amount of consumer credit. And adherents of the Consumer Credit school are not entirely insistent that such credit must at first be issued to every person from the cradle to the grave. The solution is affected by the ratio of production to the human employment it requires; and also by the precise uses to which Producer Credit is put. Credit which is devoted to the production of fixed capital certainly distributes purchasing-power in the process of building factories and erecting machine plant. And if the credit is not arbitrarily withdrawn and cancelled, it may have further beneficial effects. But considering the nature of power technique it seems that further great extensions of productive enterprises can only result in so rapid an accumulation of goods with a relative decline in human employment, that, sooner or later, some form of direct consumer credit will have to be adopted.

There is, however, one important consideration which moves the present writer towards a pronounced sympathy with the consumer credit philosophy. It is often objected against theories of monetary reform that they propose to make everyone "better off", while leaving human relations in industry pretty must as they are. We have implied that to create public power to consume the total product of industry would greatly ease the situation as between competing producers, and thus between employers and employed. Nevertheless it is true that monetary reformers have not always attempted to relate their proposals to the problem of industrial organisation. And the present writer would have much less interest in their proposals if he supposed that they would leave the managerial framework of industry untouched.

Any measure of direct consumer credit must tend to restore that human status in industry which the modern economic has largely destroyed. By giving to men some economic assurance and standing independently of any contract made with an employer, it would restore economic freedom. And free men would not long remain content to work under the present industrial organisation. They would have power to create industrial democracy, to abolish the wage-system, and to claim property in their industry, without seeking a defence in remote, bureaucratic controls. The democratic guild or corporation would be the natural realisation of their position.

Monetary reformers have too often spoken as if the mere distribution of gadgets to the multitude would constitute the Kingdom of God. We need to approach the complex issues more wisely. But it does appear that a monetary technique related to human and natural reality is an essential element in the revival of Christian social culture. For it will disperse those assumptions upon which both the economic established in the modern world and the historic secular alternatives, have been founded. To get rid of the long falsification of reality is the first necessary step to the true ordering of our social life.

THE REVIVAL OF RURAL LIFE

One essential for a healthy national life is the existence of a contented rural population, with the maximum production of food from the land. Malvern said: "We must recover reverence for the earth and its resources, treating it no longer as a reservoir of potential wealth to be exploited, but as a storehouse of divine bounty on which we utterly depend. This will carry with it a deliberate revival of agriculture both by securing to the agricultural labourer good wages and to the farmer a secure and just price. . . . The restoration of agriculture must be utilised for the revival of true community which is possible in a village as it is not in great cities. Here something can be done to start the movement away from mass psychology towards the development of personality of fellowship."

In common with every other social problem the revival of rural life is fundamentally spiritual and it is from that point of view that Canon Baker has considered it. He brings to the problem a wealth of practical experience for, though he is known mainly as a philosopher, he has been for years a village priest convinced of the crying need for far reaching social and economic reforms.

THE REVIVAL OF RURAL LIFE

By THE REV. A. E. BAKER

Rector of Moor Monkton, Canon of York

> "Italy was wearied by the long years when she had been the
> cockpit of war, and she had all but lost hope and faith. Octavian
> set himself two duties especially—to revive her ancient religion, and
> to restore profit and amenity to rural life."
>
> JOHN BUCHAN, *Augustus.*

THE relation of town to country is a major problem of social
reconstruction. It is many-sided, of immediate urgency and
of ultimate importance. Although the fact is not always in the
foreground of consciousness of the people immediately concerned or of their rulers, the town is in the long run dependent on
the country for all the necessities of life. We can put the same
fact in another way by saying that man cannot live without the
earth from which he was taken.[1]

The country feeds the town. In war time we all discover that,
although in peace time the tin-opener and the refrigerator almost
persuade us that the significant thing is that New Zealand and
the Americas feed Great Britain. But it is always true that whatever we eat, except fish, came from some farm or garden or small
holding. Even the wild things like mushrooms or blackberries
were gathered by some countryman's or countrywoman's hands
as the first stage of their journey to the townsman's mouth. And
what is true of food is equally true of clothing. Wool, cotton,
leather, bone buttons, artificial silk: they all come from animal
or plant, and their usefulness to the townsman depends on the
labour of the farmer, the shepherd, and those men of many varied
skills who are called "agricultural labourers".[2] Even the most
sophisticated "ersatz" products by which chemistry would make
modern people independent and rootless—the "plastic" coffin

---

[1] "The fundamental source of all wealth is land. All wealth is a product of human
labour expended upon God's gifts; and those gifts are bestowed in the land, what it
contains and what it nourishes. . . . Land is not a mere material resource. The phrase
'mother earth' stands for a deep truth about the relationship between man and
nature." The Archbishop of Canterbury in *Christianity and Social Order*, pp. 87, 88.

[2] Mr. Fred Kitchin says in his autobiography, *Brother to the Ox*: "I believe I learned
quite a lot from George's tutoring. He was a good all-round man, and I owe him
thanks for letting me have a go at almost every job that turned up, and I must add
there isn't another class of work that requires so many different kinds of skill from
one man as farming." Mr. Tom Wibberley says the same thing in his book, *The New
Farming*: "The farm labourer is more highly skilled than any industrial operator.
An industrial operator is required to do skilfully one job . . . but a skilful farm labourer
is required to do any one of perhaps twenty jobs."

in which a man is buried after he has eaten and drunk off "plastic" plates and beakers in an artificial world of "plastic" furniture— are possible because the supply of milk exceeds, not what the world's population ought to consume, but the effective demand for it as food.

It is commonly asserted that the families of town dwellers die out in three or four generations unless they are strengthened and refreshed by new importations from the country. It would be difficult, if not impossible, to prove this, as is obvious, and so far as I know there is no statistical evidence to support the claim. It implies a belief that life in the country is more normal and healthy for human beings than in the vast agglomerations of modern cities. It is nearer to nature, whatever that may mean. Doctors say that town life means widespread neuroses. But town life has meant, up to the present, more effective sanitation, a more varied diet, quicker access to recent discoveries about hygiene and food values, and the opportunity to use the devices by which science is making man the master of his physical environment and delivering him from the necessity of long hours of heavy and monotonous toil.[1]

The dependance of the town on the country for food and clothing means that the larger modern towns become (the more completely enormous areas of Britain and other countries are "urbanised"), the more actively productive must the rural areas become. There must be a marriage or, at lowest, a partnership, between town and country. In recent decades there has seemed to be rivalry and even dangerous antagonism between them. Short-sighted policies have been built on the assumption that their interests are in conflict, and as the number of townsmen exceeds that of farm workers by an overwhelming majority (approximately thirteen to one in Britain), parliaments dependent on popular suffrage have been only too willing to sacrifice the country to the town. Manufactured articles, including machinery, for which the small rural population in England provided little market, were exported all over the world to every non-indus- trialised country. A great deal of "surplus" capital was also exported. Exports and the interest on the capital were paid by

[1] It is a serious weakness in our contemporary political organisation that both the Labour and Liberal parties are almost exclusively urban-minded.

The seven per cent of the population in the country can hardly make up for any weaknesses in the ninety-three per cent in the towns. Poor housing almost offsets any advantage the farm worker may have through an open air life, sunshine and healthy work. No one knows whether the birth-rate in the country is higher or lower than in the towns. The infant death-rate is lower in the country, and the rural general death rate is almost as high as that in the towns. But in many parts of the country we are told that only old people are left on the land. See Sir A. D. Hall, *Reconstruction and the Land*, p. 121.

imports of food stuffs; hence Free Trade. As there was always some country or other, somewhere in the world, with a glut of some agricultural product, the British farmer was always faced by ruinous competition in some branch of his trade: hence the great depression from 1870 to, more or less, 1905. Land ceased to be a profitable investment. Farmers could not make ends meet. Labourers left the village for the towns.[1]

Gradually, of course, this policy brought itself to a standstill. The countries that used to be truly rural, and to buy the output of British factories, foundries and workshops, bought from Britain the machines to make for themselves what had previously been their chief imports. Not only did Japan and other countries cease to be the customers of Lancashire, Yorkshire and Birmingham; they became their rivals. Competition became increasingly fierce for a steadily contracting market. So the rivalry developed which at any moment might break out into actual war. And war, now it has come, must intensify this process. Britain encourages every state which is not under Axis control to build factories, make machines and machine tools, to produce munitions to win the war for freedom. So soon as the armistice has been signed these factories, lathes and machines of all kinds will stand idle, ready, easily adaptable, to make bicycles, sewing machines, all the other manufactured articles which people want in time of peace: ready, in other words, to beat British manufacturers in the world market, to keep British machines and factories idle, British workmen and women unemployed—to export their unemployment to Britain.

The rapid advance of British industry in the nineteenth century, and the almost complete failure of British agriculture in competition with cheap imported food, meant that in many of the great food-producing countries land was exploited ruthlessly to make quick profits in the English market. The United States, in two or three generations, exhausted what had taken millions

---

[1] The number of men and women engaged in agriculture (farmers, their relatives, and employees) was returned in England and Wales as just over one million three hundred and twenty thousand in 1871. The first two classes were the same, to within one per cent, in 1931, but the number of employees had dropped to almost exactly half what it was sixty years before. There were several causes for this: labour saving machines, the general simplification of the processes of agriculture, but chiefly the laying down of arable land to grass. But contrast the first-hand observation of Mr. Fred Kitchin in *Brother to the Ox*: "Every Sunday morning a group of farm chaps could be seen examining each other's ploughing, for ploughing was a fine art in those days, and the plough lads took great pride in showing of their best. It was the introduction of American diggers that killed their interest. for ploughing has no glory when done with a digger plough. Lots of good ploughmen refused to get hired to a place where diggers were used, and so drifted to town work, not because of higher pay but because they could no longer put heart or art into their work. Digger ploughs and Dutch barns—in their earlier days—drove as many good men off the land as did lower wages."

of years to accumulate, the fertility of her almost innumerable square miles of top-soil. And in the years between the wars they gathered the grapes of wrath that the pioneers and capitalists had planted.[1] Dust brought a large part of the farming of North America to a standstill; for what is true of the United States also holds for large areas of Canada. In South Africa ruthless growing of cotton and wasteful, ignorant methods of stock-raising have meant that year by year the desert gained steadily on the fertile land. And a similar story is beginning to be true of Australia. The possibility of world famine, not merely a failure to distribute what God's generosity and man's science and skill can produce, but also an actual shortage of bread, has at last risen above the horizon, even though at present it be but a cloud the size of a man's hand. It is all symbolised in the fact that during the nineteen-thirties the United States had become one of the food importing countries. This means two things. First, immediate steps must be taken, so soon as the war is over, to set up international machinery to implement the last of the regulative principles which the English Christian leaders added to the Pope's five peace points: "The resources of the earth should be used as God's gift to the whole human race and used with due consideration for the needs of the present *and future generations.*"[2] Secondly, in this country a long term policy for the revival of agriculture must be worked out with due consideration for all the interests concerned (consumers, agricultural labourers, farmers, land-owners, as well as the British Dominions and other overseas producers) with the definite determination that as large a pro-portion as possible of the food of our people, at *as high* a standard of living as we can obtain, shall be produced in Great Britain itself;[3] and this, not merely for one generation, or in view of the imminent threat of war or famine—not getting as much as possible out of the land at as little cost as possible—but restoring and preserving the fertility of the soil, "with due consideration for the needs of . . . future generations." Farmers have a saying in the North of England: you should live as though you will die to-morrow; you should farm as though you will live for ever. If

[1] "In the United States, of the total area of land under crops no less than 61 per cent—253,000,000 acres—had in 1937 either been completely or partly destroyed or had lost most of its fertility owing to erosion following wrong practices in agriculture." Sir Albert Howard in *England and the Farmer*, a *Symposium*.

[2] Italics mine.

[3] "The plain position to-day is that we import 75 per cent of our total wheat requirements, 45 per cent of our barley, and 8 per cent of our oats. And the total cost of this is between £30,000,000 and £40,000,000." C. H. Warren, in *England and the Farmer*. "In the British Isles there are fifty million people and there are forty-three million acres of agricultural land. This gives us nearly one acre per person, and who will question that one human being can be solely provided for from this area." Tom Wibberley, *The New Farming*.

we learn what that means, we shall have a policy for English agriculture.

The most urgent aim of farming is to produce as much food and clothing as possible. Food must be produced, not to make profit for farmers or rent for landowners or "employment" for workers, but to feed the people. It is part of the "natural order", as theologians and philosophers say, that production exists for the sake of the consumer. Plenty must be accepted as a good thing, and the policy of slaughtering young hogs to prevent them breeding, or burning wheat to keep up the price, must be recognised for what it is, and what W. G. Peck has called it, "an insult to the Blessed Sacrament."

As a churchman and a country parson, however, I am not exclusively concerned with the economic problem, the production of food. I am concerned with the kind of men and women that rural life produces, and ought to produce: with the good rather than with goods. I am convinced that a healthy prosperous agriculture can be the basis of a worth-while life for men and women, that it can be a vocation. Recently my daughter was in a farm-house in this parish when the farmer came in from his work—rather later than might have been expected, for he does much of the work of the farm himself. She asked him: "Do you like it?" And his answer was: "I enjoy every minute of it." The same man, on another occasion, pointed out to me that the working farmer finds his life in his farm. It is his interest and his enjoyment, his conversation in his leisure time as well as his sole concern when he is at work. It is only occasionally that a farmer goes to a "shoot", or follows the hounds: two or three times a year. Farmers read few books, go rarely to the theatre, and not often to the cinema. The steady drain of labourers to the towns, and to navvying and other work not on the farms, makes it almost inevitable that farmers come less to Church than their fathers came, even when it is not war time, with Home Guard and other practices for which time can hardly be found on any day but Sunday. Their farm is their life, and this is not, as a sophisticated townsman with a literary education might fancy, merely monotonous drudgery. To a large extent it brings satisfaction to a developed human being. But the Church may lead such a revival of rural life that it will be fuller and richer, more human, than it has been in our time.

The English rural landlords present a problem of which the solution is hard to find. They are at once impossible and irreplaceable. It is true of the best of them that, by hereditary tradition, they belong to the "place" as much as the place belongs to them. They used to have a real concern for the quality of the farming on their estates; there were clauses in the covenants under which farms were let, designed to maintain the fertility of the soil. Recent legislation, however (in Acts of 1921 and 1923) has had the effect of removing the owner's control over the farming of his land, for in practice he can be rid of an unsuitable tenant only by giving him two years rent. Nevertheless, the indirect influence of a landlord who knows his job (they ought to be trained for it as men are trained for every other "key" position in social leadership) on the standards of farming in his district is surely very great. Good landlords discharge, as no one else can, many valuable social functions. The land is theirs, so they can take long views, in their own interest. Most of them would be horrified at any claim that they have any aesthetic education, but they have a feeling for the simplicity and dignity of the villages, and for the seemliness of the buildings which give much of its character to the English countryside; and no one who has been a member of a Rural District Council can doubt that there should be some one who will be concerned that new cottages or cowsheds should not too glaringly disgrace the standards of the past or that new motor or other roads should not cut too ruthlessly through the quiet and beauty of England's green and pleasant land. Landlords who have grown up on their land can be careful, as newcomers and government departments may not be, to preserve timber and develop afforestation; and some one must do this if the land is not to be left not only sterilised and sterile but also with no beauty that man should desire it, vast ranch-like fields fenced with posts and wire, like Sir Daniel Hall's dream of heaven.[1]

Landlords can, if they will, promote rural culture in the fullest sense of the words: setting their faces against the fashion for mass-produced tools and toys and furniture, cheap foreign cotton goods, and all the beguilements of the chain-store, but encouraging a sound taste for local craftsmanship, for things made to use and last rather than to sell quickly and wear out quickly. They and their families can encourage the revival of the social and cultural life of the countryside: seeing that Women's Institutes, for example, and other adult educational movements, are led to aim at the best, in drama, music, weaving and other crafts, in flower gardens, and in social and educational life generally. The country inn, unfortunately, has passed largely out of the control of the squire and the parson. And even in those few cases where one or the other owns the inn, the beer and wine are too often a sad disappointment to any but a depraved taste.

On the whole, however, it must be confessed that these keen,

---

[1] A. D. Hall, *Reconstruction and the Land*, pp. 85–88.

competent trained landlords of whom we have been speaking have become a myth, a mere ideal uncontaminated by much expression in actual rural life. Twenty-five per cent of the farms of England and Wales, and nearly the same proportion in Scotland, are occupied by their owners. Of the remainder of rural Britain Mr. A. R. McDougall has said that 90 per cent of the landowners are not trained for agriculture and know little about it. An appreciable number own land for no other reason than that they inherited it. In most cases the death duties were paid, not by selling a few farms but by mortgaging the whole estate. And in cases in which this has been done more than once the effect in restricting the landlord's contribution to efficient farming, cutting down his expenditure on drainage, farm-roads, buildings, and so on, is too obvious to need mentioning. Many successful stock-jobbers, newspaper proprietors, barristers, politicians and novelists buy rural estates for the social prestige that goes with "a place in the country", and care for nothing but the house, the garden and the view, and, perhaps the hunting, shooting and fishing. Hunting is a pestilential nuisance. Not only is it the last refuge of that worst kind of snobbery which encourages people to be idle without shame and cruel without remorse, but it interferes with food production in more ways than one. Shooting, also, is neither innocent nor harmless. And it cannot be denied that all over the country agricultural land is bought and managed and let to tenants not in order that the maximum amount of food shall be produced, but for sport and pleasure.

It is sometimes pleaded that the landowner cannot do what he would like to do for the land because of the heavy national and local charges on it. But the fact is that the special needs and rights of landed property are at least adequately recognised both in rating and also in taxation. The death duties on land are between 30 and 40 per cent lower than on any other form of inheritance. And agricultural land pays no rates whatever. The fact must be faced that the benefit of the derating went, almost entirely, not to the tenant farmer but to the landowner; the value of the land went up by exactly the amount of the derating. Indeed, all the so-called gifts to agriculture—not only derating but also the subsidies on wheat, beef, milk, and sugar beet, amounting in all to well over £40,000,000 per annum —are gratuities to the landlords. Rent, Sir A. D. Hall reminds his readers, is the margin between what the land can earn and the living wage that will induce the farmer to carry on. He adds "At the outset the tenant probably is allowed the benefit of the remission (or subsidies) in order to made his fallen income up to the standard expected. But even that saves the landlord from a remission of rent."[1] The truth is, I fear, that since the death of Queen Victoria the standard of expenditure of fashionable "Society" has risen by so many hundreds per cent that the very small annual interest yielded by land, considered as an investment, so far from being returned, as most of it should be, to provide equipment for agriculture, has been spent off the land altogether.

Almost all students of the subject—politicians, economists, sociologists, agricultural scientists, and even, very reluctantly, farmers—are agreed that the only solution of the problem, and the first step towards a healthy and prosperous agriculture is the nationalisation of the land: of agricultural land, primarily, but justice demands that the compulsory state ownership of farms shall be accompanied by similar control of urban land and that needed for other uses. The Archbishop of Canterbury (Dr. Temple), indeed, said in 1940 that the rural landlord discharged many social functions, and that the nationalisation of agricultural land would work out very badly; he even used the word "disaster". In his recently published Penguin, *Christianity and Social Order*, however, he has arrived at the view that the existing rights of landlords are excessive if social function is taken as the justifying correlative of rights of ownership. He thinks that the landlord-tenant relation is likely in any case to decay. But he had stopped half way on the road to national ownership, at the hope that that occupying ownership, "where a man owns land which he works himself and works land which he owns," can be made to work.

The objection to "owner-occupier" as a general solution of the urgent problem of removing the present agricultural distress is, however, easily stated. Already about a quarter of the farming land of England is owned by those who farm it, and they are not, on the whole, a success. The surveys carried out for the County War Agricultural Committees prove that most of the worst cases of neglected farms—buildings in disrepair, fencing and drains neglected, the land under-farmed and understocked, its fertility exhausted—are to be seen in owner-occupied farms. Many of them bought their holdings at the close of the last war, were obliged to take out a mortgage because the purchase price was ridiculously high, and since then have escaped bankruptcy, perhaps, only by putting as little into the land and taking as much out of it as they could. It is significant that the Archbishop and Captain McDougall, from whom his Grace gets comfort and encouragement in this matter, couple with their vote for owner-occupiers a strong caveat against their being allowed to mortgage their farms.

[1] *Reconstruction and the Land*, p. 44.

No! The only way out from the present impasse is by way of State ownership of land. Lord Addison, the best Minister for Agriculture the country has had for a generation, declares, as a result of an expert inquiry, that to take the first steps in a restoration of British agriculture will need an expenditure of £250,000,000, for the provision of suitable buildings, good farm roads, and proper equipment for the feeding and care of live-stock. Additional money must be found for drainage and water supplies. This is not a vast sum, as modern expenditure goes: it would not maintain the British war effort for a month. But it is hopeless to expect the farming industry to raise it. And it is equally hopeless, as well as wrong, to expect the nation to raise it unless it were for the improvement of land and the development of an industry which will belong to the nation and supply it with an important part of its food. Not only so, but those friends of agriculture who have once accepted the idea of the nationalisation of rural land see at once that it will have the additional advantage of removing many other obstacles to the full development of farming.[1]

There would be very strong resentment among farmers, of course, at any suggestion that the nationalisation of rural land should be accompanied by "farming from Whitehall",[2] the control of farming by some soulless government department, making the agriculturalist responsible to some routine-ridden civil servant who has spent his official life perfecting systems of office procedure and whose chief end would be to make farmers fill up forms and answer questions. This need not be, however. The land that belongs to the nation can be farmed by farmers, with security of tenure and the kind of equipment and the long-term and patient help which the State landlord can afford.

What will be lost and missed when the private landlords disappear is the initiative and leadership which the best of them have provided for the rural community. All who know and love country life and long for its restoration speak with enthusiasm of the service the landowners have given.[3] When they go, as apparently they must, the natural leaders of the new rural democracy we hope to create will be the parson, the schoolmaster (or school-mistress) and the doctor. These will have to be better than they have been, and a new, more populous village

[1] Lord Addison in *Programme for Agriculture*, pp. 44 f., and other writers in the same volume (Michael Joseph, Ltd.).

[2] Mr. A. J. Hosier, world famous as a pioneer in successful farming, wrote in *Programme for Agriculture*: "Agriculture is such a unique industry, incomparable with any other, and there always seems to me to be an element of irresponsibility about land managed by a man whose income is safe whether the farm is financially successful or no."

[3] See Sir A. D. Hall, *Reconstruction and the Land*, pp. 69, 70.

5

life will attract a better type. The rural areas have had a very poor deal, both from Church and State. Only very rarely (so far as I know, in one training college only) is any particular provision made in the education of elementary teachers for preparing them for work in village schools. And the fact that the salary of a head teacher depends on the number of children in the school means that, except in rare special cases, the country gets the teachers the town does not want. It should not pass the wit of man to devise a system under which country-born men and women shall be encouraged to find their vocation in helping to fit boys and girls for life "on the land". It sounds dull, but it may be thrilling; it is the foundation without which there cannot be a better world.

And, in the same way, there must be a more suitable sort of country parson than there has been during the present century. The life of the country priest, seen close up, does not look particularly attractive. Probably he has a house and garden too large for him, and an income too small for them. He is almost compelled to spend too much of his time gardening, after a not too successful fashion, and his wife and daughters become household drudges. Two things are wrong. The Church has decided neither what kind of life it expects its ministers to live nor what kind of man a country parson ought to be. Are they to be simple, godly, educated men sharing, with their households, the lives of the poor in homes in which the poor can feel welcome, or are they, as at present, to hang miserably suspended in an intolerable limbo between what their training has encouraged them to think of as the heaven of comfortable affluence and the hell of more or less genteel destitution? They are as isolated and friendless as any section of the community; would-be gentry, but the gentry are not on visiting terms with them and the people never dream of going near them unless they have some particular reason for doing so. The country parson who knows his people best is usually the man who is half a farmer, and is knowledgeable about pigs and turnips and manures; sometimes, not always, he is not so devout as he might be. Often, however, the priest who is diligent to maintain a daily Eucharist, prepares his sermons carefully, and aims at making his visits spiritual opportunities, has little contact with the minds of his flock because he does not understand their lives.

Who are the country clergy? A certain number of them are diocesan officials, given the charge of small parishes so that they may have time for committees and other service for the Church at large. Some are scholars, or at least students, who seek leisure to read, and perhaps write, but live in a world of which their parishioners know almost nothing. Some have worn themselves out in large, understaffed urban parishes; to them a country benefice is more than semi-retirement, but they cannot be expected to provide the initiative and understanding leadership without which there will be no uplifting of rural life. A considerable proportion of county clergy are there because they are not fitted for town work. Only a tiny minority, however, are country priests because, so help them God, they could no other; in other words, because that is the life for which they were born, and in which, all frustration overcome, they can find scope and satisfaction for the powers and graces that God has given them.

On the one hand, in the past, able, good and holy men have been content to be country parsons. On the other hand, the Church can provide, as no other institution can hope to do, stimulus, sanctions and opportunities for men and women who would serve God and fulfil their vocation by producing food. The Eucharist has its unstrained meaning more obviously in a country church than anywhere else. The fellowship of mutual and common service is seen without difficulty in a village parish where, even now, most people who live in the place have some contact with the church. I shall have more to say about that on a later page. At present it must suffice to recall the fact that it was the Lutheran Church which, by its spiritual and intellectual initiative, made possible the agricultural revival which had made the Denmark over-run by Hitler world-famous for its bacon and dairy products.

Farming in Britain can be made to pay. Given security of tenure, reasonably fixed prices, and the capital the State would be justified in expending on the industry, it can produce a very large proportion of the food of the population (some authorities say, far the larger proportion). And agriculture as a revitalised industry, with villages again centres of progressive life, and the crafts and industries that would arise to depend on it, would provide wages and a healthy, happy life for a million and a half or two million people. The "hard core" of permanent unemployment could disappear. Not only so, but another problem would prove capable of solution. Already I have hinted that after the war there are bound to be acute difficulties in the export trade for manufactured goods. The Americas, South Africa, India—rapidly and increasingly—will manufacture all they need. There will be, there must be, large-scale unemployment in the towns of Britain—factories, mills, foundries, coal-mines will be idle—unless we have a populous and prosperous countryside. If farmers and farm workers have money in their pockets and ideas in their heads, the shopkeepers will be busy, the industry of Britain will be active and healthy. Unavoidably, there will be fewer imports, because fewer exports. We shall have to learn to live by taking in each other's washing. It may be a more simple, less flashy, less luxurious life. But it will be our own. Britain must aim at being self-supporting, if only because the way of sanity is to produce food and goods to supply your own need, to live on what you produce, and to sell the surplus. It is just insane to work primarily to make and grow things to sell, and to try to live by buying things with the money you get in return.

All the experts—practical farmers, economists, agricultural scientists—are agreed that Britain can be made, ought to be made, a great food-producing country. Much of the land to-day is under-farmed, some of it is poor and "out of heart", its fertility exhausted. But even recent experience, that of the last twenty years, shows that men who are trained and wide awake, and have control of sufficient capital, can make farming a success. It would be unnecessary standardisation and centralisation, however, to assume, because state ownership of land is the first step to the recovery of farming, that one aim must dominate all farms and one method be imposed on all farmers. There is an amazing variety of soils in Great Britain, and it stands to sense that different kinds of land are best for different sorts of product and that, other things being equal, the land that is best for corn should be used for corn, primarily, that best for meat and dairy products should be used for them. Where soil suitable for market gardening is found near urban areas it would be vain to miss such an opportunity. But, on the whole, if the fertility of the soil is to be maintained, and even more where exhausted land must be restored, there should be a rotation of crops, with roots (and sheep to feed off them and manure the land), grassland for dairy herds, but grassland often ploughed up and having its place in such a rotation.[1] Speaking of the ploughing campaign of these war years, Mr. A. G. Street has said that the good grain crops followed the ploughs of the good grass farmers. Lord Addison believes that by adding five million acres to the land that was arable before the war, and by improving eight million acres of grass, our output of wheat could be raised at once 114 per cent, the milk output doubled, the meat increased by 25 per cent, eggs by 50 per cent, and fruit and vegetables more than doubled.[2] And we could and should do more than that. There need be no fear of a surplus of food that could not be consumed. In the

---

[1] See, for example, Sir R. George Stapledon and William Davies, *Ley Farming* (a Penguin Special). To a layman in agricultural matters there seems much that is valuable, also, in *The New Farming*, by Tom Wibberley.

[2] *Programme for Agriculture*, p. 83.

seventies of last century, for example, when large supplies of cheap American cereals began to pour into Denmark, the Danish farmers were not content to be ruined by that competition; on the contrary, they used the cheap corn to feed pigs and cows. Plenty of corn again, if Britain and the world can grow it, may mean not only enough bread, but lots of meat, eggs and milk, that is, a high standard of living. It is only in a country where consumers are poor that most of the wheat needs to be eaten as bread. There is no need to fear a glut of agricultural produce in Britain, still less in the world as a whole. The investigations of Sir John Orr have shewn that a considerable proportion of our population have been tragically under-nourished.

The best soil in Britain should be let as "family farms", between 50 and 150 acres each, to be worked with little hired labour by the farmer and his wife and their sons and daughters. Such people are strong and independent, alert and careful (the eye and foot of the master are the best treatment for the land); and because they are always aware of their dependence on Nature, they have a simple piety. A community in which the number of family farms is considerable can be healthy, sane, keen, cultured, human. The wife, on a family farm, plays an important part in the home, and is a real partner in the running of the business. Hers is the feeding of hens and poultry and calves, a share in milking, the making of butter, bread, pickles, jam, the curing of ham and bacon, cheese-making, plain and fancy sewing, and other handicrafts. She becomes expert in many kinds of skill, and women's institutes in such communities are real cultural associations where technical knowledge is pooled and minds and skill are developed. Children, also, are real helpers—and their bodies, minds and characters grow—in the work of such a farm. They find interest and health and spiritual development in caring for animals, as in other parts of agriculture. Young farmers' clubs are, in the long run, more satisfying than night clubs and dance bands and cocktails. Quite often, indeed, a community of small farmers and their families attain a social and cultural life which is dignified and simple, and quick with intelligence. An England in which such things were encouraged and multiplied would have a solidity and independence and fundamental unity which would provide the stability we shall need in the chaos of the post-war world.

Most of the agricultural land in Britain, however, is not good enough, and has not been sufficiently well looked after to be fit for that kind of farming—let in such small farms it would not provide a living for a family. If the second class land is to be equipped and restored to play its part in a national revival of agriculture, it must be by large scale farming, fully mechanised, with alert attention to the most up-to-date researches on agricultural science. Farms of this sort will give scope to first-class men with training and initiative to manage them and to young men with keen minds as their assistants. And they will employ more men on land which is not of the best, and in spite of the use of machinery, than could be absorbed by the old-fashioned traditional methods applied to smaller farms. Lord Addison has said that something like half the agricultural land in England has been under-farmed, and it is to that land that this large-scale method must be applied. There are, of course, two standards of efficiency in agriculture. Sir A. D. Hall says that the test is not the amount produced per acre, but the amount produced by one man's labour; in 1938 in Britain the gross output per man was £380, and the net output £285. But if the test is to be not exclusively economic but rather human and social also, we must face the fact that before this war we had an average of three men per acre employed on the land, Denmark had six, and Holland and Belgium had about ten. And Lord Lymington says that "a family working a little holding for subsistence, and getting its main income from a local craft and summer work on larger holdings, will produce far more food per acre than the big factory farm."[1]

Can farming be made to pay and, if so, why has it not paid during the last two or three generations? Farming has failed, farmers have lost heart and their banking accounts have melted away, because of what is euphemistically described as "unstable prices". Again and again the bottom has dropped out of the market, so far as the things the farmer has to sell are concerned. He has to plan months ahead, and he has had no guarantee that after ploughing, sowing, harrowing, reaping, threshing, the price he will get for his produce will pay a reasonable profit. And the same thing has been true of his livestock. Farming has been a gamble because of the absolute uncertainty as to prices. And the first requisite for putting the industry on its feet is guaranteed prices. Mr. Hosier has put it plainly: "The most direct method of increasing production is to make the market price sufficiently attractive." That means two things. First, the farmer must be protected from the unreasonable and organised greed of the "middle man", the distributor. As Lord Cranworth has said:[2] "It has been not only possible but common for the man who distributes the milk from his depot to the consumer to receive a higher remuneration than the man who buys or breeds the cow, feeds, houses, and doctors it, milks it twice or thrice a day, and

[1] *Programme for Agriculture*, p. 110. [2] ibid., p. 176.

finally transports that milk to the distributor's depot." And at a meeting of the National Growers Association in Leeds the secretary complained that prices are fixed, in the Ministry of Food, by wholesalers, not by growers. The result is that, e.g. the grower of tomatoes gets 9d. a pound, and the distributor 7d.— an entirely unfair proportion. Secondly, the farmer must not be subjected to the competition of uncontrolled imports—from a country where there happens to be a glut of wheat, or apples, or mutton, or from a country where exports are subsidised by government, or from a country where wages are inhumanly low. During war time, in the national interest, competitive capitalism and free buying and selling have had to go by the board. Prices have been "pegged" by the Government. The wholesale price has been fixed at a level to make it possible for the ordinary, intelligent hard-working farmer, on any land which it is in the national interest to farm, to pay a reasonable wage to his workers and to make a reasonable profit for himself. Partly for this purpose, imports have been controlled by Government. And the retail price of food has been fixed at a level which people generally can afford to pay. It does not seem to me unreasonable that so far as food and other necessities are concerned this amount of control, and of limitation of liberty, shall be continued after the war. Before the war the breakdown of capitalism was marked precisely by its failure to distribute the goods. The symptom was: poverty in the midst of plenty, plenty causing poverty, plenty considered as a bad thing, plenty destroyed in order to keep up prices. It was impossible for the producer to escape bankruptcy if the goods were marketed as a price the consumer could afford to pay. But it should be an axiom for Christian thought that plenty is a blessing, the product of man's labour expended on God's gift, the means to a full human life worthy to be offered in worship to the Giver of all good. So that it will be the condition of a healthy agriculture after the war that the farm worker shall have wages and conditions comparable to those of the urban worker, that the farmer shall have a fair profit for a reasonable amount of thought and work and capital. This means a guaranteed wholesale price, and the preventing of price cutting. The retail price, also, should be fixed by the Government, so as to encourage ordinary people to buy as much food as a generous and varied dietary suggests. The difference between these two fixed prices—wholesale and retail—should, as at present, be paid by the taxpayer. This, however, may be largely relieved if all imported foodstuffs are bought by the government at the prices ruling in the world market and sold, in some cases, at a profit.

Where are the workers to come from for a restored agriculture? How is the drift from the country to the town to be stopped and, indeed, reversed? It is part of our case that what are called agricultural labourers are, in fact, skilled workers: shepherds, ploughmen, hedgers and ditchers, the men who build stacks and thatch them. These have largely disappeared. Doubtless many of them, however, could be attracted back again. There is, in any case, a widespread belief that many who have tried the towns, and have not done too well there, are disillusioned and would readily return to farm work if the prospects were good enough. First, there must be better houses for farm workers; a conservative estimate is that 250,000 are needed at once. There must be some attempt to build the new cottages in hamlets or villages (loneliness had driven women to refuse to live in the country), near a school and a church or chapel and a 'bus route, considering the convenience of those who live in them at least as much as that of the employers. And they must have the decencies that people in towns expect and that even in the country professional men and "gentry" take as a matter of course: electric light, water laid on, sanitation and a bath-room. And there must be reasonable prospects of advancement for men who choose farm work; up to the present it has been practically impossible for a farm labourer to become anything more than the smallest of smallholders; which is one reason why a lad with "anything about him" will not go on to the farm. Most modern boys are mechanically minded, and it should be made clear to them that the new large-scale mechanised farming will offer scope and a healthy life to people with that kind of taste.

The education offered in rural areas must be (it *ought not* to need saying) a preparation for rural life. Town-bred teachers educated in towns and trained for town work who, moreover, have their friends and spend their leisure among people with urban ideals and standards are a positive danger to rural life. They themselves take it for granted that blackcoated occupations are the way to and mark of success in life; and the Local Education Authorities and His Majesty's Inspectors judge teachers by the number of scholarships they win to urban secondary schools. The whole authority of the educational system, never mentioned because it is assumed, is a contempt for rural life and habits and ideals. I hope for the time when the Board of Education will consider it a qualification for an inspector in a County area that a man has been born and brought up in the country, and when, equally, the village school will not be like the town school, except that it is worse, but will have a life and curriculum integrated into the interests and needs of the community of which it forms a part. If children are to be taken from small village schools when they are eleven, the Central schools to which they are transferred must not merely have a rural bias in the sense of teaching modern methods for poultry, pigs and dairying, but also be planned to prepare for the kind of rural community we have envisaged. They must teach motor-engineering as well as joinery and the other village crafts, and not be afraid of agricultural science. The new farmer must be encouraged to overcome his inherited suspicion of theory and research, and learn to make the most of his land and of himself. In this connection it would be worth while to take a leaf from the notebook of the Danish High School movement, and encourage young men and women up to twenty-one years of age to work on the farms during summer, from seedtime to harvest, and return to some farming college or county institute during winter.

Every movement for a fuller and more adequate education ought to be able to count on the encouragement and guidance of the Church. Far more than "religious instruction", in the narrower sense of the word, is the concern of the clergy and of the faithful laity. All that helps, or may be used for the full development of personality is our business. So long as children have to be content with a mere smattering of teaching about *facts* (mathematics confined to the simplest arithmetic, history little more than lists of kings and dates, literature never ambitious to rise above mediocre verse and trivial prose), and so long as they leave school before they have awakened to appreciate beauty or truth, or anything beyond the more conventional aspects of goodness, it will not be surprising if they never get to the point of seeing what religion and civilisation are about. The Church in the country areas must give an energetic lead, not only in demanding facilities for technical education in agriculture and other rural works, but in all those communal activities which teach people, without saying it, that the "useful" is not the only thing which is worth doing, and that living is more than a living.

Life in the country and agricultural work are steeped in religious motives and hopes; they are *naturaliter Christianae*. To the understanding, unperverted heart they preach the Gospel of Creation. Man is and is not a part of nature. It was made for him. But was it? Have you said the whole truth about the brute creation when you have described his dinners, his pets, and his servants? And what of tigers and crocodiles? When man as master of nature exploits it merely for his own profit the relation proves itself essentially false and abnormal by the fact that it degrades man instead of improving him, "waging an impious warfare with the very life of our own souls". Health and happiness come when man is not nature's lord but nature's priest, when, that is to say, the dependence of the creation on the Creator becomes in man conscious, free, deliberate, responsive and grateful. All this must be canalised and even, in the proper sense, defined in the worship of the Church. As men offer with glad hearts themselves and their lives, in every relation and function, to the Father and Creator, they give Him His own from whom all good things come.

The production of food is an essentially Christian activity, for since Christianity is the adoration of the living and true God, it is the most materialistic of all religions. This business of food and feeding is, of course, profoundly mysterious. As Gilbert Chesterton once remarked, it humbles a man to recognise that his life on earth would come to an end but for "sticking alien substances into a hole in his face". Food represents vividly and unforgettably the truth that no man liveth to himself. No more than any other organism can be isolate himself from that which is not himself. At least, if he does so, he dies. And the work of producing food, also, convinces a man, at every stage of the process, that he is not and cannot be *autonomous*. When he has done all that he can, and done his best, the result is beyond his control. The soil is not his creation; he cannot make a living germ; and although he can foretell the weather for a few hours ahead, and large scale human activities modify it to some small extent, on the whole weather is a brute fact which has to be accepted for what it is:

> When God sorts out the weather, and sends rain,
> Why, rain's my choice.

The principle enunciated by St. Paul will always hold: Paul planted, Apollos watered, but it is God that giveth the increase. The farmer has to wait and hope and trust that the Power by whose life we live, working through the order of nature, will not fail. Where the Church consecrates and encourages this natural piety it always wins a response from unsophisticated people. The sanctification of nature's year is of the essence of the Gospel. It is a pity, therefore, that the revival of Plough Sunday and Plough Monday was left to the initiative of Trade Unions, but Rogationtide services and processions, although modernists would hardly allow us to pray for seasonable weather, take the Faith into the farmyards and the fields, and Harvest Festivals need not fear the sneers to which some Anglo-Catholics subject them. The Church must consecrate and inspire the daily round, the physical task, lest they become trivial and ordinary or, worse, degrading, deceptive and unsatisfying.

As I have said elsewhere, the physical universe is permanently an inspiration and strength and discipline to a man only when, quite definitely, it is the means of his fellowship with God. The vague sentimental nature-worship of the spring poet gives a delusion of nature's sympathy, while men are willing to be deluded. But it is only when they experience the natural world as the means by which the Father of spirits reveals Himself that men find real courage and satisfaction in contact with nature. Their apprehension of nature's loveliness and their recognition of natural order can mean only that they share, with whatever finitude and imperfection, in the mind of God. And the darker side of man's intercourse with nature, also, the terror and cruelty and waste and suffering are not entirely intolerable because they express God's will that men should, through the use of and conflict with these things, attain the freedom and full personality through which alone they can have fellowship with God. They are "the shade of His hand, outstretched caressingly." So the Church must be in the countryside to remind the farmer and the labourer to pray. Their Father knows that they have need of these things before they ask Him, but do they know that they need Him? If we forgot God it would be worse for us than if we were hungry. The evils of life—from "poverty in the midst of plenty" to the wars which it must inevitably produce—come from forgetting God.

The Eucharist especially must be so re-ordered and newly emphasised that common men may find in it the sanction and Christianising of the toil by which they earn their living and serve the community. There, in the Father's House, the economic life of His children is offered to Him to become—not what it is now, the occasion of and almost overwhelming temptation to greed and competition and hatred—but the opportunity and channel of redeeming love. It is a Table for all, provided by the brotherhood, that every member as he partakes of it may discover the Body of Christ, in the community of which all alike may learn to be, may grow to become, brothers gaining "from every man his due service, for every man his due reward, that each may live for all, and all may care for each."

This chapter may be summarised by way of conclusion. Our first aim must be to feed the people of Britain; not a minimum sustenance, but plenty to eat, varied and attractive. Our second aim must be to produce as much of the food as possible on our own soil. There must be a revival of agriculture, and to that end we must plan a prosperous and well-populated countryside. The land must belong to the people, i.e., to the nation, so that the nation's resources, in no niggardly fashion, may be used to provide equipment and all other facilities for good farming. The farmer must be guaranteed a wholesale price that will make him able and willing to give of his best in thought and knowledge and work, and the labourer must be assured wages and conditions which will make him willing to give his life to the most ancient, most skilled, most honourable of all industries. That means that Government must control imports. But if there is to be a market for the food and goods so produced, the distribution charges, and retail prices must also be controlled, so that producer and consumer both shall live and be happy. And religion and education, varied, free, and as good as they can be provided, must enrich and discipline and humanise the life of the agricultural community, that men and women and children throughout the countryside may have the health and happiness and freedom of God's open spaces and the civilised amenities that two thousand years of Christian Europe have taught us that man ought to have. Is it an idle dream? I am comforted by these words of Lord Addison's: "There is no sufficient reason why our villages should be half deserted and half decayed; why half our land should be covered by poor herbage, yielding poor support for scanty flocks and herds, why land that is by nature fruitful, should be waterlogged and derelict; why dilapidated building should disgrace our countryside; why experienced cultivators should be exposed to recurring distresses arising out of no fault of their own, or why people, who in times past have been the stalwarts of our race, should feel compelled to turn away from what might have been a life of fruitful labour and the best content."[1]

[1] *Programme for Agriculture*, p. 87.

WHAT SHALL THE NEW ORDER BE?

The last three essays are devoted to the consideration of how the Malvern aspirations can be translated into action.

Both Sir Richard Acland and Mr. Sidney Dark go much farther than Malvern in their condemnation of the profit-making basis of industry and Miss Kenyon, who writes most persuasively and with expert knowledge of Christian Corporatism, and Mr. Dark, who writes as a convinced Socialist, are fundamentally opposed. It is the scheme of this volume to include these different points of view of people, equally concerned for the creation of a saner, kinder and juster society, with the object of encouraging personal consideration of the tremendously difficult problems of progress and reconstruction.

All three writers have had in mind a new order in which not only will there be economic security for all with adequate incomes and good housing, but in which the spiritual freedom, vital for the good life, will be assured. This spiritual freedom has been denied to the majority in the old order, it cannot exist in a totalitarian state, and as Mr. Dark admits, it may be hard to secure in a Social Democracy.

The Malvern declaration is: "Every citizen should have assured liberty in the forms of freedom of worship, of speech, of assembly and of association for special purposes not contrary to human well-being: such freedom implies for every citizen not merely the exercise of a right, but much more the fulfilment of a responsibility."

The great task is to secure "this freedom" in the coming political and economic arrangements and it is not to be forgotten that one devil may be driven out only to make room for a legion of devils.

WHAT SHALL THE NEW ORDER BE?

THE CASE FOR COMMON OWNERSHIP

By Sir Richard Acland, M.P.

Late in 1940 some eight individuals of what are generally called "progressive" views, were seeking some basis of common agreement. Each in turn described the sort of society he would like to see. Professor John Macmurray spoke last. "Before you decide where you want to go," he said, "it is advisable to find out, if you can, where you are in fact going."

This is important advice.

It is no use wanting to go north if the force of the world events, as well as all the present and all the possible future currents of public opinion, have irretrievably committed you towards the south. If you ignore these forces, or fail to understand them, then at best your endeavours will be wasted; at worst, by confusing good counsel, you will assist the bad.

This is not a denial of the existence of human freewill, or an argument in favour of predestination. Individuals and groups, by their wisdom or their folly, courage or timidity, honesty or selfishness, can deflect and shape the course of events. But only within certain limits.

From a moral point of view the limits are extremely wide.

It would be an exaggeration to say that in the next fifty years we have a choice between unlimited good and unlimited evil; for we cannot be so optimistic as to hope that in so short a time all evil can be eliminated, nor need we be so pessimistic as to fear the destruction of all good. But it is no exaggeration to say that in these years we can make a greater moral advance or a greater moral retreat than in almost any other similar period in our history.

On the other hand, from an economic point of view, the choice is extremely narrow. There are not many different economic shapes in which good or evil can come to us in these next years. And the most evil shape would be in many respects remarkably similar to the best.

For example, those who are arguing for a return to unlimited *laissez faire* are arguing for an impossibility. Those who extol the virtues of a society in which every man is, or has the prospect of becoming, his own master are arguing for something which cannot be. Those who would like to substitute individual craftsmanship for the conveyor belt are working against irresistible forces.

If all the people who want these things were to form themselves into a political party, and were to have at their disposal all the finest orators, all the best organisers, and unlimited finance, they would still fail in their objectives.

Humanity has found, in the vast factories such as the Morris works at Cowley, a means of production far more powerful than all the million workshops of the individual craftsmen. At no time in the next fifty years will the big factories be abandoned.

Looking inside one of these factories we will find it quite possible to allow to each man the right of making his suggestion on points of detail, and to take part in a democratic discussion of policy in general. But the very shape of the factory itself requires that detailed administrative policy must be in the hands of a comparatively small executive—say at most 1 per cent of all those employed. This means that 99 per cent of those employed cannot under any circumstances be their own masters. They must fit themselves into the main plan for the factory as a whole. Whether we are ultimately ruled by autocrats, bureaucrats or democrats this must be so.

Then look at the factory in relation to the economic development of the country as a whole. Consider the small executive committee which controls the detailed administration of the whole concern, and holds in its hands the factory's vast productive power. Whoever appoints this executive, to whomsoever they may be ultimately responsible, the days are gone when they can take the decisions relating to their factory without conscious reference back to the total economic policy of the community.

The forces which are binding these factories together in ever greater industrial and financial units are irreversible. From first principles we can feel sure that there is no way of compelling two factories to compete with each other for our benefit, when they have decided to combine with each other for their own. And this theoretical conclusion is confirmed by experience in America where "trust busting" has been much more seriously attempted than in Britain. A recent careful Congressional Report has shown that in spite of persistent governmental efforts to the contrary, the ultimate control over an ever wider field of American economic life is steadily passing into the hands of ever fewer and fewer individuals.

These considerations confine our economic choice within comparatively narrow limits. Whatever we do, and no matter how hard we may struggle for an opposite result, we are going to live in an industrial community whose major policy is consciously and centrally planned, and within these narrow economic limits there is a very wide moral choice. For the major plan may be directed by the representatives of the many, for the benefit of the many, or by the representatives of the few, for the benefit of the few. Within the same narrow limits, and within the framework of the economic plan, it is possible that each individual will live his own life for high and generous motives. It is also possible that each individual and group will be struggling against the others for individual self-advantage. And finally, within the same economic framework, the generality of men may or may not believe in God and direct their lives to His service. Nor will it ever be easy for us to distinguish the steps which may lead to the best results from the steps which must lead to the worst. For of course every advocate of every proposal will always claim that it will produce benefits for the many, and will lead to an unselfish way of life.

The proposals which will be put forward, however, will divide themselves, economically speaking, into two main groups.

On the one hand there will be proposals, differing from each other in detail no doubt, but all in the last resort calling for a complete and fairly early transfer of all the substantial productive resources of the country from private ownership to common ownership. On the other hand there will be proposals, once again differing in detail, under which, while one or two individual industries may be nationalised, the great bulk of our productive resources will remain in the hands of private owners over whom there will be exercised some form of public control.

If I am asked therefore what are the inevitable basic economic and political developments within the limits of which we must struggle "Towards a Christian Order", I would reply that we are committed irretrievably to a situation in which we will have to make our decision between common ownership, and public control over private ownership.

This conclusion is of the utmost importance to us; particularly so, because many people to-day are conducting their thinking as if the issue before us were something entirely different. Indeed there are many people to-day who, thinking that the issue lies between unrestricted individualism and complete socialism, ask us whether it is not possible for us all to agree on a compromise in some form of public control over private ownership.

At first sight this will seem extremely reasonable, and those who believe in common ownership will be accused of intransigence when they do not agree. But if it is understood that unrestricted individualism is an alternative which has already been ruled out, not by our conscious decision, but by the force of events, then the matter appears very different. For it then becomes clear that those who ask for public control over private ownership are in fact saying: "As I want one thing and you want another, can we not compromise on the basis of your agreeing with me?"

Unfortunately for those who would like to see for us a political future without any fundamental divisions of opinion, with no political parties, and with everybody co-operating to work out the best detailed application of fully agreed principles, no such compromise is possible. The issue will have to be faced.

If this is the issue, what is to be the position of Christians? Are we to be neutral, or are there any Christian reasons for preferring one side to the other? I believe there are, and I do not think we can afford to be neutral.

But I must offer one word of warning. Up to now I have written quite dispassionately. I have even tried to write scientifically, seeking for facts without any personal bias in favour of the conclusions so far reached. But from now on I write as a partisan. It is my own very keen personal desire that the cause of common ownership shall prevail, and the reader must therefore check my arguments much more carefully before he accepts them.

Let us assume an attempted public control over private ownership. Each factory, or group of factories, belongs to a private owner or group of owners. These owners, or their nominees, exercise some measure of control over the major and minor activities or inactivities of the factories which they own. They receive an income out of the balance sheets of these factories, and this income is larger or smaller (or may indeed become negative) in accordance with the varying states of these balance sheets.

Now some public authority—that is to say some group of men ultimately responsible to our democratic Parliament—is seeking to exercise some measure of control over these privately-owned factories, so as to assure that the results of the total activities of all the factories is to promote the general well-being of the community as a whole.

It would seem to be a comparatively easy thing to control the private owners so that if they want to do something which is contrary to the public well-being they shall be prevented from doing it. Suppose, for example, a shortage of building materials; and suppose that while some private owners are willing to build modest houses, others are anxious to build a block of luxury flats. In these circumstances it seems not too difficult to introduce a licencing system which will prevent them from building the luxury flats.

But it is extraordinarily difficult to "control" private owners so that they shall positively do the things which ought to be done when they do not want to do them.   Thus if no one wants to build houses of the kind that are required, no methods of *control* will cause them to do so.   On the contrary, by subsidy or otherwise, it becomes necessary to create the conditions in which they will find it worth their while.

But this matter goes much further.   When the decisions to run or not to run the factories, to expand or to contract the scale of their operations, are taken by private owners whose individual incomes depend on the results of their decision, then the total national economy will only work to its full capacity when the private owners as a whole are satisfied (or as they put it "feel confident") that conditions as a whole are conducive to their earning some profit on their proposed operations.   There is no way of "controlling" them into feeling this confidence; it is necessary to create the conditions in which they *do* feel it.   And as the control of our major industries passes into the hands of smaller and smaller groups, the leaders of these groups, meeting together, will find means of informing the community what these conditions are.   And, acting collectively, these men will be quite capable of letting the community know that they, the arbiters of our total economic destiny, will not feel the necessary "confidence" until such time as the government has reversed the general policy which "we" elected it to pursue but which "they" dislike.

It thus seems to me inevitable that as long as private ownership of our principle resources remains, no attempted public control over it will succeed, since the most powerful private owners acting together will form a power within the state, stronger than the democratically elected representatives of the community as a whole.   I do not say that this is universally true of private ownership in all societies at all times.   But I do believe it to be true of the particular industrial society which must inevitably exist in this country for at least the next fifty years. And if it is true, it means that the major plan for the community will be made inevitably by the representatives of the few.

It is not, of course, certain that under common ownership the major plan will be made by the representatives of the many. It is possible that it will slip into the hands of an unscrupulous and irremovable political caucus.   But unless we propose to despair of democracy (which is after all a brand new instrument of human government still in its experimental stages), we surely ought to be able to hope that the British people will retain the means of ridding themselves of some little gang that directs their resources contrary to the will of any substantial majority.

Let us now consider the position of the individual.

Speaking to all sorts of audiences and to all sorts of people in the last twelve months I have found amongst them an amazing unanimity in deploring the low moral quality of our ordinary working lives during the years between the two wars. I am not ignoring the doctrine of human sin, nor am I suggesting that we can do things merely because we want to do them. But I am sure there is amongst our people now a deep longing *to be enabled* to live a more generous life.

It is my very earnest conviction that against the background of the inevitable physical development of our economic and industrial machinery, private ownership of the great productive resources, however it may be controlled, makes the generous life permanently impossible.

This is a vitally important point. It is the very core and centre of my beliefs for the future, and I must endeavour to elaborate it at some length.

Beneath the almost inarticulate longing for the possibility of a more moral daily life, there lies the hard stark fact that for at least a hundred and fifty years we have consciously sought to develop our whole communal life without any moral foundation.

Our community has been devoid of any moral purpose. We have thought it permissible to allow, and indeed to encourage, and indeed to oblige, each man to promote his own self-interest. To promote one's own self-interest may not be an immoral purpose, but at the best it is a non-moral purpose. We have assumed that we could, without hurt, build up our community on this non-moral foundation because we supposed that if each pursued his own advantage, the total results of the endeavours of each must be to promote the maximum well-being of all. Religion ought, from the beginning of the nineteenth century at least, to have challenged this assumption as a matter of principle. It did not do so. If we have not now learned, as a matter of practical experience, that the assumption is false, I do not know how many more disasters humanity must encounter before we learn that we cannot live without a moral social purpose.

What, then, can this moral social purpose be?

Frankly I do not find this question so very difficult. Indeed I have the feeling that many of our present social thinkers are, unconsciously no doubt, pretending that this question is a difficult one because they do not want to face the next question which will arise when this question is answered. Agreeing that we must in fact find a moral social purpose, they seem to suggest that we must postpone all but the very broadest of decisions on all further problems until some exceptionally penetrating thinker can tell us what this social purpose is to be. Admitting that I may be a fool, I propose to rush in where others fear to tread.

We must live our ordinary daily working lives in order to serve our community and to see our community itself as the servant of less fortunate communities.   This answer is so obvious as to seem almost tautologous.   And yet what other answer can there be for the whole of our community to-day?

Some will say at once that the answer is inadequate because we will not succeed unless we live our ordinary daily working lives in the service of God.   I will agree with this objection to this extent, that unless there are a sufficient number of people who are living their lives in the service of God it is doubtful whether we will in fact produce the kind of society in which service to the community can become our moral social purpose. I use the word "sufficient" because it would be over-optimistic to hope that all people could soon live for the service of God. If this is so, then the moral social purpose which I have described is the only one which can simultaneously include those who do, and those who do not (or do not yet) believe in God; and it is therefore the only moral social purpose which we can adopt as the basis of such part of our thought as relates to communal economic or industrial policy.

The really difficult problem, from which I believe many contemporary thinkers are trying to escape, is this: What must we do in order that this may indeed become the moral social purpose of our community?   My answer to this question is that we must end private ownership of the great productive resources of the community.

Now I have already warned the reader that he must treat me as a partisan and check my arguments with care.   I must now also warn the reader to treat himself as a partisan and to check his own reasoning with care.   For unless the reader has already accepted my conclusions, very powerful forces within himself will seek to dissuade him from doing so now.   In part this arises from the fact that "the old arguments for Socialism" have been effectively in front of the reader ever since he developed the powers of political thought.   Therefore, if he did not accept these arguments for Socialism then, to accept my arguments for common ownership to-day may seem to amount to an admission of error.   This is psychologically painful.

Furthermore any decision is mentally painful.   Indecision is an attitude of mental rest.   We allow ourselves to hope that the burden of decision may be removed from us.   We allow ourselves to believe that a little more waiting, a little more discussion or research, a little more collection and correlation of the necessary facts and data, a little more expert advice, will produce some higher synthesis of public opinion in which the burden of taking a decision which other people may oppose will be removed from us. If we have decided that the very fundamentals of our present situation impel us to an acceptance of common ownership, then when we are presented with one of the serious problems which will arise under the new form of society, this problem becomes a heavy burden which we have to bear, knowing that we will have to work out its solution. But if we have not yet made our major decision, then this problem is no burden to us at all; we merely by-pass the problem by pretending that it is one which will not arise because, after a few more weeks or months delay, someone is going to give us a major solution to our difficulties which will make its solution unnecessary.

I believe that the fundamentals of our present situation do impel us to make the psychologically burdensome decision in favour of common ownership.

Unless we are prepared to say that our civilisation can continue without any moral social purpose, then we have to ask how it is possible for men to live their daily working lives primarily for the service of the community when the facts are that the first result of their doing so with real generosity will be to benefit, not the community, but their particular owners?

If, every time I work harder, or more conscientiously, or more intelligently, or with more initiative, the first result of my doing so is to benefit some individual owner of the resources upon which I am working, then I am bound to think of my own work first and foremost in terms of what I am getting out of it for myself. If, on the other hand, I am working on resources which are, in one way or another, owned by all of us in common, then I may work first and foremost for the service of the community.

No one ought to disagree with the conclusions I have reached unless he can either say that we do not need a social moral purpose, or can say that he believes the generality of men can work first and foremost for the service of the community when they are working on resources which are owned by private individuals.

Those who do not accept the conclusions will probably be unable to make either of these assertions. In my experience they do not generally seek to controvert the argument which I have advanced in any way. They will more usually say: "Yes, your argument is quite right, but, human nature being what it is, we cannot yet dispense with the profit motive."

This answer arises from a confusion of thought in the definition of profit motive. Profit motive has two distinct meanings, a broad and a narrow. And it seems to me that people are led by their knowledge of human nature to insist that we cannot yet dispense with the profit motive in its broadest meaning, and then, by the mere accident that we happen to use the same word in a different sense, they assume that we are therefore prevented (until we have changed human nature) from ending the profit motive in its narrowest meaning.

In its widest meaning, the profit motive operates whenever there are in force any arrangements by which the man who does more work, or more skilled work, or more responsible work, receives a higher income than the man who does less work, or less skilled work, or less responsible work. But in its narrower sense the profit motive exists when certain men, by virtue of their ownership of property, enjoy a personal income which arises out of the difference between the cost of production and the sale price of the goods or services which are produced out of the property which they own; and when these same men exercise some rights of decision over the policy to be adopted in relation to this property, and relate their decisions to the probable or possible effects which the decisions will have upon their own income.

One day, when human nature is something very different from what it is to-day, and very different from anything which it might become in any reasonably short space of time, we may hope to abolish the profit motive in its narrow and in its wider sense. Common ownership requires that we shall abolish the profit motive in its narrower sense in relation to all the substantial productive resources of our community. Common ownership to-day does not require that we shall abolish the profit motive in its wider sense at any near future time.

Under common ownership we can preserve and almost certainly improve the piece rate system for many different forms of activity. We can widely adopt the system of group bonuses. To preserve an enterprising spirit within the major direction of our total communal endeavour we can certainly set targets for our leading production managers and technicians and offer bonuses either to groups or individuals if these targets are passed or attained. We can offer direct financial or other material reward for any work which has outstanding merit.

Nor will we expect the individual, in his work, to be unmindful of the direct material advantages which he will win for himself and his family by high individual endeavour. But, as the whole system by which endeavour is related to reward will be coherent and intelligible, it seems to me not impossible that each man, in his working life, will subordinate his hopes for individual reward underneath the motive of working in the service of the whole community. Indeed one might almost say that the impossibility of finding the social moral purpose within the structure of private ownership arises from the incoherence and unintelligibility of the whole system relating to endeavour and reward.

In order to deal with this matter in yet greater detail I would like to consider it in relation to one or two particular problems, and I would like to take first the problem which arises when an individual worker sees that the particular job on which he is engaged could be done more economically. Let it be assumed that he is working with five men and sees how the same job could be done with four.

It is surely a common place that we desire, incidentally, to produce a situation in which the individual man feels that his own ideas are of consequence to the whole community, and in which it will be easy and natural for him to bring them forward. It is not easy or natural under private ownership for a man to bring forward "economical" ideas such as I have described.

To begin with, if the man we are thinking of, and his five colleagues have been receiving seventy shillings per week, whose seventy shillings was it before it was theirs? Before the seventy shillings became their wages it was, indisputably, the property of "the boss", and it is immaterial whether the boss is an individual owner or a more distant set of shareholders.[1] Thus it may be pretty talk to make out that the seventy shillings is the reward which the community gives to the worker for his service to the community. The stark facts which emerges into the life of the individual workman is that his wages are paid to him out of the private property of "the boss" and are given to him for working for "the boss".

Under this system, what is the position of the individual worker who sees that his job could be done by four workers instead of five? If this fact becomes known, one worker will cease to work on this particular process. It may be pretty talk to show, in the terms of the classical economists, that this change will set in motion complicated forces which, if they are not checked by any tendency towards monopoly control, will result in the greater advantage of the community, and in the employment of some worker to replace the man who is thrown out of work. But the fact that emerges into the life of the individual worker is that he, or one of his mates, will be stood off from the particular job he is doing, that there is no guarantee that the private employer, or any other employer, will find a job for the man who has been stood off, and, above all, that the boss will be getting the same

[1] Where there is an individual owner who maintains close personal relationship with his men these personal relationships may partially counterbalance, or more than counterbalance, the adverse considerations which I am describing. But they never eliminate them—they are there all the time—just as a two pound weight will remain in the left hand scale even when a three pound weight, placed in the right hand scale, causes the balance to tip from left to right.

job done as was being done before, and will be seventy shillings per week better off.

Under common ownership, on the other hand, the very money which comes to a man as wages will be the community's money. It will represent the fact that the community rewards him for his service to the community. The benefit of his suggestion will go directly to the community; the community itself will be getting the same job done at seventy shillings per week less cost; and the community, having this seventy shillings, is automatically provided with the means of employing the worker (superfluous now for the old job) on some further work of general advantage. It thus becomes possible for the individual worker to feel, in his daily work, that he is working to serve the community.[1]

I will offer a further, and more personal, example, to try to illustrate my point. I happened to be sitting up all night on telephone duty with a man who had been a bricklayer, and we had a very long conversation. I do not pretend that in what follows I am giving the exact words that were used on either side. But I am giving the general sense of what we said.

MYSELF: "I would like to ask you about the trade union restriction on laying bricks. It can be regarded as a piece of organised selfishness, and it is a question whether it ought not to be brought to an end."

MY FRIEND: "It works out in this way. Of course I can lay more bricks than the trade union rate. Say I can lay twice as many. My mate may be able to lay half again as many. Suppose we do so. As we are on piece rates, the first thing is that I

---

[1] It will not be possible for me, in the course of this contribution, to develop at appropriate length the argument which forces me to the conclusion that there *cannot* be unemployment under common ownership. I have tried to elaborate the point adequately in notes to be found at the end of two books, *The Forward March*, and *What it will be like*. I feel obliged, however, albeit in the form of a footnote, to offer an answer to the man who asks why the spirit which I have described does not animate the Post Office and the Royal Ordnance Factories.

The advantages which I claim for common ownership can only materialise when the new system makes possible a new atmosphere throughout working life as a whole. This new atmosphere will not be achieved except through many forms of education, preaching and propaganda which only become possible when common ownership is the standard background of our national life. To-day the general atmosphere of working life is determined by the conditions of private ownership. We are prevented from even trying to make the propaganda for communal service which common ownership makes possible. It is this atmosphere which is taken from the world of private ownership even into those parts of our present system which are operated under common ownership. And this tendency is reinforced by something more. The workers as a whole think of themselves as "we" (i.e. the ordinary people) who are working for "them" (i.e. the men who run the show). *And they identify the government of the country with "them".* Government money is not "our" money, it is "their" money. Thus the men who are working in the Royal Ordnance Factories, are, from their own point of view, just as much working for "them" as the men who are working for Vickers Armstrong. And it is only when we alter the totality of our economic life that we will be able to begin to try to introduce a new and a healthier atmosphere.

get twice as much money and he gets half again as much. But the next thing is that someone says we are laying far more bricks than before, and my mate gets turned off. Then they come to me and tell me that my job seems to be much easier than they thought, so they decide to re-rate the job in such a way that for double the number of bricks I may be getting 10 per cent more than before.

"Now what is the total effect of all this? No more bricks are being laid. My mate is out of a job. I'm getting 10 per cent more than before. But the boss is scooping the difference. That being so, the trade union restriction will stay."

MYSELF: "Then I would like to present to you an entirely different conception of our whole community. Supposing the brick-fields and cement works were ours, so that no one made a good thing out of cement or bricks; supposing all the land were ours so that no one made a good thing out of ground rents; supposing the very enterprises which were organising your building works were ours, so that the only effect of your laying more bricks would be that your fellow men would get their houses quicker, then what about it?"

MY FRIEND: "In that kind of community, believe me, the job would be perfectly easy."

Now it may be that even under the present system some other individual bricklayer might have been persuaded that the restriction on the number of bricks should be abandoned for the sake of the community. But I am absolutely certain that it is not possible, within the framework of the existing system, for bricklayers as a whole to elect a trade union secretary who will be in favour of its abandonment. The very shape of society—and specifically the operation of its principle resources for the private profit of individual owners—prevents, in the generality of men, the development of the moral social purpose which is now necessary to us.

Many have excused themselves from an open acceptance of this conclusion on the grounds that even an elementary understanding of the principles of Christianity should assure us that no changes in the physical structure of society can automatically produce saints. This must arise from a misunderstanding of the argument itself.

It is no part of the argument to suggest that a change from private ownership to common ownership will automatically produce for us the social moral purpose which we need, or that it will, in itself, persuade even a single man to live his life generously to the community instead of selfishly.

Although the system of common ownership will give us a coherent and intelligible relation between endeavour and reward, it is freely admitted that human selfishness may produce, within this system, a set of men who will cheat and wangle for the better paid positions which they do not deserve. It is further admitted that the whole society may turn out to be governed by a power-hungry political caucus, just as our present system is governed by a power-hungry economic and financial caucus.[1]

All these things will only be prevented if in fact we do succeed in developing new moral standards for individual and communal living. This will not be done except through the united endeavours of all those who perceive that it must be done. In fact we need to conduct now a moral, spiritual and religious mission to the British people.

It is not my case that our transfer from private ownership to common ownership will guarantee the success of this mission. It is my case that this transfer will give the possibility of success to this mission. And it is emphatically my case that so long as we retain private ownership of the great resources this mission cannot even begin—except, of course, in the hands of those who are also simultaneously advocating the need of common ownership with the utmost possible vigour and with no possibility of misunderstanding.

Unless this mission succeeds, our new society will fail. For my part, I cannot see how this mission can succeed unless a sufficient number of people are persuaded to live their lives in the service of God.

There are those who believe that the whole task can be accomplished on the basis of humanism. It is not easy to convince them that this is not so; for to these people living one's life in the service of humanity appears to be a sufficiently inspiring and a sufficiently compulsive ideal for our purpose. I doubt whether these people sufficiently realise that if we accepted their view there would be nothing behind our community more inspiring or more authoritative than a leaflet or a lecture from the Ministry of Information.

I have no doubt that these leaflets and lectures could be very well produced. We could call in aid the whole of our educational

[1] It should, however, be noted on this point that our present political democracy does give to our people as a whole the very machinery which they require in order to remove a tiny political caucus which governs contrary to their will, and unless we propose here and now to despair of democracy for which we are fighting, we ought to have enough faith in ourselves to be reasonably sure that such a caucus could always, in the last resort, be removed. As against this there is no machinery whatever by which the people as a whole, under private ownership, can rid themselves of the economic and financial caucus however much they may dislike the policy which it pursues.

system, as well as the whole power of wireless, stage and screen. Through all these agencies we could tell our people that they would all be much happier if they would all conscientiously serve their fellow men.   The humanists must tell men that they would be happier; they cannot tell them that they will be better, because they have no criterion by which good can be measured.   And although their argument might carry some weight when addressed to a public meeting, its weakness lies in its failure to convince the individual.   The individual may readily admit that individuals will be happiest in a community in which all serve their fellow men, and he may agree that such a community is the best kind of community for himself to live in.   But he receives no authoritative or compulsive answer when circumstances suggest that he himself would be happier still if he broke some of the reasonable rules of society for his own personal advantage.

In order that this socially destructive temptation may be resisted with some chance of success it seems to me essential that a man should sincerely feel it to be an essential part of his religion not to yield to it.

For these reasons, writing as a politician, I entirely agree with those ministers who have been telling us with great consistency that no political schemes can save us unless man will believe in God.

I would, however, ask ministers of religion whether there is not a true converse to this truth.

If belief in God requires that men shall live their daily lives generously towards their fellow men; and if there is something in the very structure of our society which makes it impossible for men to live their lives generously; then men will not believe in God unless those who say that they believe in God are vigorously attacking that which makes it impossible to live generously.

I am aware that this may not be true of all men.   In particular, it may not be true with those who have not yet seen the need of playing their part in the struggle for a more tolerable shape of society.   But most of our alert citizens to-day are deeply anxious to play their part in the struggle for a more tolerable shape of society.   And it is right that this should be so; for our whole experiment in democracy would otherwise be meaningless.   From my own personal experience I can testify that many of our citizens who are most anxious to live their lives as conscientious democrats cannot even open their minds to the possibility of belief in God unless those who believe in God are attacking the structure of society which makes the generous life impossible.   I can further testify that many have in fact been brought to a belief in God through their contact with some of the relatively few but spiritually powerful ministers of religion who are already working to this end.

Summing up, then, what I have written, I believe in the near future that we will have to choose between common ownership and some form of attempted public control over private ownership.

Under common ownership I regard it as possible, but not certain, that the major plan for the development of our economic life will be made by the genuine representatives of the many; that the generality of men will live their lives for the necessary new moral purpose; and that a sufficient number of men will believe in God.

Under private ownership, however controlled, I regard it as certain that the major plan for the development of our economic resources will be made by the representatives of the few; that we will be held firmly clasped to the self-centred way of living; and that no sufficient number of men will be won for a belief in God.

For these reasons I most sincerely hope that those who contend for common ownership will prevail. Weighing the political forces as carefully as I can, it is also my very strong opinion that they will prevail—possibly even within the next two or three years, and almost certainly well within the life time of most of those now living.

I believe that Christians acting as such, and acting in their capacity of ordinary citizens, should assist in bringing about this result. They should do this firstly because it is morally right and will promote the widest possible belief in Christianity. But they should also do it because the new society which we will seek to build will need the authoritative teaching of Christianity if it is to achieve good results. And Christianity will have no authority in the new society if Christians, as such, have done nothing to bring the new society into being.

CHRISTIAN CORPORATISM: A NEW GUILD SYSTEM FOR INDUSTRY

By Ruth Kenyon

CORPORATISM has at the moment a bad name among us, because the Dictatorships everywhere have arrogated to themselves the name of Corporative States, and have organised their industries along what they claim to be corporative lines. In fact, however, of the three essential characteristics of a genuine corporatism, Totalitarianism caricatures the first and contradicts the other two. Corporatism means first and foremost that industry becomes organic to the community, part of a functional order of society. But totalitarianism makes it a function not of society but of the State. To reduce it, or rather to promote it, to functionalism of any kind is indeed an advance upon the order of capitalist industrialism, which left it a merely buccaneering, profiteering adventure. So far Fascism must be given credit for restoring the idea of purpose to economic life. It has perceived what Mr. Peter Drucker has called "the End of Economic Man", the complete disillusionment, frustration and self-contradiction which has descended on the civilisation which acknowledged no common purpose and expected all good to follow on the pursuit of material goods. But the purpose round which Fascism sets out to organise the life of society is an incomplete and inadequate purpose, the mere power of the State. The other two elements in a genuine corporatism are the relative autonomy of each corporation, its responsibility for doing its own job in its own way; and the membership in the corporation of every person concerned in it, workers and managers as well as investors, freely organised in their own units. These two demands are essential if the corporations are to be part of a truly functional society, which implies the free functioning of every part in an integrated whole. But there is no freedom, and therefore no real responsibility, in the Fascist corporations, which are tied to the State and the Party. Though they incorporate a Labour Front, with certain strictly limited rights over against the employers, the employer-employee relationship remains; wage-labour remains; the property of the capitalist in plant and profits remains. In short, the industrial order of a totalitarian State is a State-dominated capitalism. Moreover, so far is Fascism from having effectively ended the apotheosis of economic man, that it declares that only in his occupation has a man any claim to representation in the State.

For a Parliament representing the citizen the Fascist State has substituted a Chamber representing the Corporations. It is worth noting, however, that in Portugal, where Salazar is attempting to found a Christian Corporative State, this final indignity has not been inflicted, and a National Assembly stands beside and above the Corporative Chamber.

Thus it is altogether a mistake to identify corporatism with Fascism, or to suppose that Fascism invented the idea which Christians have attempted to criticise and transform. Precisely where Mussolini got his conception seems to be unknown; but it was much more closely related to the State capitalism which had for some time been developing in Germany than to the National Guilds idea which arose in England in the decade 1910–20, and was the outcome of syndicalist criticism of collectivism as affected by reflection on the functionalism of medieval society. Similar forces also worked contemporaneously in the Catholic social movement on the Continent, and produced a theory which culminated in the pronouncement of the encyclical *Quadragesimo Anno* of 1931:

> As things are now, the wage system divides men on what is called the labour market into two sections resembling armies, and the disputes between these sections transform this labour market into an arena where the two armies are engaged in fierce combat. . . . This opposition should be done away with, and well-ordered members of the body social come into being anew; vocational groups, namely, binding men together, not according to the position they occupy in the labour market, but according to the diverse functions which they exercise in society.[1]

Following on this, the *Semaine Sociale*, annually held by French Catholics, devoted its session of 1935 to the whole question of Vocational Groups. Evidently desiring to distinguish Catholic doctrine about them from the Fascist Corporation, its report[2] declared:

> That the Vocational Group is not to be identified with the State. The State will give a charter to the Vocational Group, but it does this not as creating the authority of the Vocational Group. . . . The State recognises the authority of the Vocational Group and confers upon it the necessary legal powers without either absorbing it or supplanting it.

And

> The words Corporatism and Corporative State are ambiguous and should be avoided. The individual is called to develop his life

---

[1] *Quadragesimo Anno*, Catholic Social Guild translation, p. 38.
[2] General Conclusions of the French Social Week held at Angers, 1935, quoted in the C.S.G. booklet *The Guild Social Order*, 1936, pp. 52 ff.

in the family, the local community, the province, the Vocational Group, and the State.

The Vocational Group is something quite different from and much greater than a voluntary association; it should be compared rather with a municipality. All are as free to choose their professions as their places of residence, but none may evade the public authority, whether of the town or of the profession, which has been set up for the good of all.

It is thus the inherent authority of the group, as a natural and freely functioning organisation, on which the *Semaine Sociale* report lays emphasis. Moreover it adds that the existing voluntary occupational associations should be the nucleus of the chartered and responsible groups it envisages:

> Common sense obliges us to avoid doctrinaire preconceptions. There are already existing institutions which are embryo elements of Vocational Groups, especially the Trade Unions and Employers Associations, which are the provisional government of professional society in process of organisation.

In the same sense the Rev. Ch. Raaijmakers, S.J., LL.D., lecturing to the Catholic Political Party of Holland in 1928 (and thus before the publication of Pope Pius XI's encyclical), says: "According to Catholic principles the State is not a machine but an organism. . . . This means not merely that all the parts must work harmoniously together and are co-ordinated, but that they are autonomous as far as the general interest will allow. . . . The productive activities of the community ought to be directed towards satisfying the needs of all the people . . . [but] production at the present day is organised only on the principle of gain. . . . The worker is not reckoned as a co-operator in production, but as the supplier of a commodity the price of which is determined by demand and supply." It is indeed the business of the State, which has the oversight of the general good, to intervene to end this immoral condition of affairs, but not by exceeding its function and superseding the authority of the groups properly charged with the organisation of industry. It must intervene "by the creation of organisations which represent the two groups of industrial partners, employers and workers, and by gradually handing over to these organisations the control of those matters which are their proper concern."[1]

Again, the Rev. A. Muller, S.J., Doctor in Political and Social Sciences, speaking in 1935 at a meeting of the International Federation of Christian Trade Unions, and representing Belgian Catholicism, says that industry must cease to be regarded

[1] The lecture is printed in translation in the C.S.G. booklet already quoted.

from a purely individualistic point of view, as a mere livelihood, a means for income and profits. It becomes a function fulfilled for the good of society, and all who follow it . . . must combine their efforts and control their activities for the benefit of their trade and of the community. . . . Professional or corporate organisation becomes, then, an obligation binding upon all in the name of the common welfare. . . . It belongs to the State, as protector of the common good, to give effective recognition of this obligation and to endow the corporations with the rights and privileges necessary for the complete fulfilment of their social function. . . . But authoritarian methods, hastily applied in the dictatorship countries, far from favouring a sound corporative system, have rather endangered its working and development.[1]

These rather numerous quotations are cited for the purpose of showing that the idea of a revived functional social order is neither proper to totalitarianism nor yet the conception of a few faddists in this country. It is the recognised industrial doctrine of Catholic sociology, and that definitely in the form of a free functionalism incorporating the workers' free associations, not in the Fascist caricature of these. This makes it the more significant that the Anglican Christian Social movement, working as it has done quite independently of its Roman Catholic opposite number, has been led to emphasise similar points in its Christian criticism of current industrial anarchy, and as represented by what is probably its most coherent doctrinal development, the Anglo-Catholic Summer School, to formal acceptance of the functional idea as its constructive policy. To go so far back as the Arch-bishops' Fifth Committee Report, 1919, not only did this declare "that it is precisely the general economic organisation of society which is, in some respects, defective," and that the necessary "fundamental change" should aim "at making the spirit of co-operation for public service the dominant motive *in the organisation* of industry" (italics mine). It put first and foremost in its critique "the peculiar and, as we think, unjustifiable position of subordination in which many wage-earners are placed . . . the position of economic inferiority in which . . . the worker is liable to be placed by his dependence for his livelihood upon an under-taking whose general policy and organisation he is powerless, as an individual, to control. . . . The conditions of their work may be determined not by them, but for them, and may be deter-mined by the financial interests of persons who are responsible neither to them nor to the community." This second point, of responsibility to the community, is further developed later in the Report. "Industry is a social function. An industry, when all is

[1] ibid., pp. 17 ff.

said, is based upon the association of men to obtain a livelihood by providing society with some service. . . . Its relation to the community should, therefore, be one of subordination to public needs, and it realizes its purpose in proportion as those engaged in it do not endeavour merely to obtain the most advantageous terms for themselves, but take a pride in providing the best and most economical service which they are capable of rendering . . . the temper of loyalty and mutual confidence which springs from a life of corporate endeavour and achievement."

The Lambeth Conference of 1920 put its finger, if less forcefully, on the same points: "Whether or no the demand for the full 'democratising of industry' is practicable or even reasonable, it is at least clear that the workers in an industry ought to have an adequate share in the control of the conditions under which their work—a large portion of their life—is carried on." It quotes Dr. Westcott's dictum that "wage labour . . . is as little fitted to represent finally or adequately the connection of man with man as in earlier times, slavery or serfdom," and in the well-known Resolution 74 declares, in phrases which were not at that time *clichés*, that the necessary "fundamental change in the spirit and working of our economic life . . . can only be effected by accepting as the basis of industrial relations the principle of co-operation in service for the common good in place of unrestricted competition for private or sectional advantage." It mentions "Guild Socialism" along with Nationalisation and Labour Co-partnership as possible methods for creating the desired new order.

In 1930 Lambeth regretfully recorded that "we cannot yet say that society has even yet come to believe that industry exists for man, not man for industry." It reaffirmed the resolutions on social and industrial questions passed in 1920, with special emphasis on No. 73 (condemning the pursuit of "mere self-interest") and No. 74.

It is on this background of persistent discontent on the part of the Church in this century with the whole economic structure and purpose of contemporary society that the English National Guilds movement falls to be considered. The series of quotations recording this discontent may be concluded by two admirably relevant sections of the Malvern Report. No. 17 states that

> The proper purpose of work is the satisfaction of human needs; hence Christian doctrine has insisted that production exists for consumption; but man is personal in all his activities and should find in the work of production a sphere of truly human activity, and the doing of it should be for the producer a part of the "good life" and not only his way of earning a livelihood.

6

No. 23 runs as follows:

> This status of man as man, independently of the economic process, must find expression in the managerial framework of industry; the rights of labour must be recognised as in principle equal to those of capital in the control of industry, whatever the means by which this transformation is effected.

Historically, it was the National Guilds movement of the decade 1910–20 which in this country gave form to the idea of a functional structure for industry and its full democratisation. Like so many other enthusiasms of the war period, it faded out, for the time being at least, under the pressure of post-war conditions. But while it lasted it was an extraordinarily interesting example of the work that can be done by intellectual leaders in impressing a form upon, and so stimulating the effectiveness of, existing tendencies in the working-class movement. What would now be called the Left party in the Labour world was about 1910 swayed by the influence of the French Syndicalists. Both in France and here, Syndicalism was a reaction against mere collectivism as an expression of the Socialist ideal, and in this country also against the concentration of energy on political activity. The first had received a severe shock when an allegedly Socialist Minister, Briand, broke a strike on the French National Railways, just because they were nationalised and a public service, by the device of calling up their employees in the character of conscripts, who could then be ordered as soldiers to operate the lines. The second, after all the triumph which greeted the arrival of a Labour Party in the Commons in 1906, was proved to be at best a long-term policy, incapable of achieving immediate results. The French Syndicalists, partly inspired by Sorel's theory of the necessity of violence, declared for the immediate capture and control of the factories by their own workers. In England, the Syndicalist group, with the veteran leader Tom Mann at its head, called for a return from political to industrial effort, and a development from the steady, largely insurance methods of the craft unions to the industrial union, backed by less money and using the weapons of the strike and the tightened belt. In fact from 1911 to 1914 there was a period of industrial unrest and numerous strikes, sometimes on a considerable scale.

The English labour movement from the days of the Christian Socialists onwards has never been out of touch with two interacting groups which have helped it to understand and develop itself, groups of intellectual theorists and of Christian prophets of social justice. In this second decade of the twentieth century it was most pronouncedly in the National Guilds movement that

these influences took shape. Its members welcomed the Syndicalist urge for a working-class activity making claims upon the rank
and file, demanding individual and local and workshop initiative,
a widespread activity fit to counter that appalling phenomenon,
the mass-man, to which the ever-increasing flood of mass-
production tended to reduce humanity. On the other hand they
perceived that unless this initiative was directed to something
constructive, not to mere outbreaks of violence, such confusion
would ensue as did actually ten years later in Italy open the
door for Mussolini and the first Dictatorship. Hence their conviction that the work must be done through and not against that
great construction of the English working class, Trade Unionism.
The Trade Unions must be made conscious of a destiny leading
them to become the instruments, not merely of collective bargaining whereby to achieve improvements in wages and conditions
of labour, but of an "encroaching control" by which capitalist-
industrialism should be transformed into an industrial democracy.

The aspiration after a revived Guild organisation of industry
came as far back as 1906, from Arthur Penty. It arose out of his
experience of the frustrations imposed on his own profession,
architecture, by commercial standards and pressures. His book,
The Restoration of the Guild System, called attention to the contrast
between the care of the medieval system for standards of work
and standards of life with the carelessness of capitalism about
either. The idea simmered in the mind of that brilliant critic and
journalist, A. R. Orage, of the *New Age*. It coincided too with
the speculations of another fertile thinker, S. G. Hobson, prominent among the younger man who were trying to convert the
powerful Fabian organiastion from a dessicated collectivism to
something capable of effecting a genuine alteration in the status
of the worker. Under the stimulus of the Syndicalist *réclame* in
1911, Hobson wrote a series of articles for the *New Age*, energetic-
ally supported by Orage as editor, demanding an end of wage-
slavery, partnership status for the workers, and the development
of the trade unions into instruments and expressions of that
achievement.

Meanwhile another of the younger Socialists, G. D. H. Cole,
Fellow of Magdalen College, Oxford, in the process of studying
The World of Labour for the purpose of producing the book under
that title which he published in 1913, had established contacts
all over that world. Thereby he both convinced himself of the
immense possibilities of Trade Unionism, and brought himself
into a position to influence its policies. He, too, demanded that
it should move forward to claim a recognised share in the government of industry, and that socialist energies should be transferred

from the advocacy of collectivism to that of guild socialism. Maurice Reckitt, who had at this time returned to Oxford with the intention of writing a thesis on early Communist writers, soon laid that aside in order to throw himself, along with Cole, and with a group among whom W. Mellor and W. N. Ewer stood out prominently, into the elucidation of a detailed theory of what Guild structure in modern conditions must involve, and, from 1915–20, into the energetic propaganda of the National Guilds League. It was Reckitt in particular who held always in the forefront of the movement an insistence on the respect due to, and the responsibility which should be thrown upon, the ordinary individual man. It was this which to him was the special attraction of the Guild idea, or the functional order, as he had learnt it in his historical studies under Dr. Barker and later saw it defined by Dr. Figgis, and later again by R. H. Tawney. To his mind, this had been characteristic of medieval Christendom precisely because it was Christendom, and consequently he not only urged it upon the propagandists of the Guilds, but urged the claims of the National Guilds movement on the Church. To him it is chiefly due that a functional order of society became from the first one of the chief concerns of the Anglo-Catholic Summer School of Sociology.

The outcrop of quite numerous actual Guild experiments in the years 1920–22 is almost forgotten now, but it was not without significance. The Building Trade gave birth to most of them, though there were other examples. S. G. Hobson and Malcolm Sparkes were specially prominent in their stimulation. Mr. Sparkes, indeed, had already ni 1918 succeeded in organising a Building Trades Parliament, fully representative of both employers and operatives throughout the industry, avowedly seeking to transform the trade into an instrument of public service. As one of its sub-committees reported[1]:

> We have glimpsed the possibility of the whole Building Industry of Great Britain being welded together into one great self-governing democracy of organised public service. . . . We believe that the great task of our Industrial Council is to develop *an entirely new system of industrial control* by the members of the Industry itself—the actual producers, whether by hand or brain—and to bring them into co-operation with the State as the central representative of the community whom they are organised to serve.

The Report, however, proved to be meat too strong for the majority of the "Parliament" to swallow, and it ultimately lapsed into something more nearly resembling the ordinary Joint Industrial Council sponsored by the Whitley Report.

[1] Quoted in Reckitt and Bechhofer, *The Meaning of National Guilds*, pp. 274 f.

Of greater significance, though equally evanescent, were the
local Guild experiments. They sent a thrill of new hope through
reforming circles of the moment, because they witnessed to an
energy of purpose and a revolt against proletarian status among
the workers themselves. Wherever a Guild came into being there
was an end of ca'canny, a readiness for self-sacrifice. and obvious
joy in good work; there was, in short, a sense of liberation. The
brief but beautiful period of proliferation began with a suggestion
by S. G. Hobson to the Operative Bricklayers' Society of Man-
chester,

> that they should solve the housing deadlock and assure their own
> freedom from capitalist control by allying their labour monopoly to
> the credit of the local authority. The idea had only to be pro-
> pounded for its significance to be instantly appreciated; the brick-
> layers found immediate support from their fellow Trade Unionists in
> other branches of the industry, and their Trade Unions being
> debarred from actually entering into such contracts themselves, they
> formed a joint authority, which they boldly christened a Guild, and
> approached the municipality with an offer to build 2,000 houses.
> Within a few weeks their concrete experiment in Guild principles
> was being discussed in every quarter of the country. . . . "Manchester
> has a chance," said the *Manchester Guardian*, "apparently a good
> chance, of carrying out an experiment which is not only of the first
> practical importance in the life of the city, but, if successful, might
> well mark a turning point in the industrial development of the
> country. That is a large claim to make, but it can hardly be put
> lower."[1]

About 140 local Building Guild Committees were formed up and
down the country, and even so far away as in America and New
Zealand, and just half that number succeeded in obtaining contracts to a total value of nearly £2,000,000.[2]

If it be asked what the Guilds did about the raising of capital,
the answer is that they did various things. The original Man-
chester idea was that the Guild undertook the contract on terms
of cost price (at Trade Union rates) plus ten per cent to cover
overheads, plant and salaries, and also (most important) continuous pay for all operatives during the period of the contract.
The municipality was to supply all materials on the spot. Later,
the Co-operative Wholesale Society offered its assistance and
credit. Later again, Guilds raised capital on their own account.
Mr. Sparkes urged that the Builders' Parliament should, through
a National Building Guild organisation, arrange for the whole
business of supply and capitalisation, including "the regular
development of real craftsmanship by the holding of continuous

---

[1] Reckitt and Bechhofer, op. cit., pp. 279 f.
[2] S. G. Hobson, *Pilgrim to the Left*, p. 224.

exhibitions of individual works of art throughout the country . . . to promote such a revival of the building art as has not been seen since the Middle Ages."[1]

It was, however, financial difficulty, aggravated by the economic troubles induced by the deliberate process of currency deflation at the end of 1920, which mainly defeated the Guild movement. Further, the centre of enthusiasm, the National Guilds League itself, was disrupted about this same time by the sweeping of its members into the rising Communist movement on the one hand, and into the Social Credit criticism of the whole financial system on the other. Labour, after struggling through the pit of that first post-war deflation to the high spots of the first Labour Government in 1924 and the near-General Strike of 1926, fell into a soured disillusionment resulting from the failure of both of these. Then came the period of mounting and continuous unemployment and the crisis of 1931, and then the new pre-war preoccupations. These two decades were no time for generous constructive social experiment. Social services, just to keep the wolf from the door, were alone in favour, whether the wolf were seen as the wolf of semi-starvation, or in the form of Bolshevik revolution.

Nevertheless, a movement on the scale of the National Guilds movement does not come and go for nothing. The Shop Stewards movement may have come into being chiefly as a form of the Communist cell, but at all events it kept alive the Guildsmen's policies of Encroaching Control and Workshop Democracy. Readers may have noticed that the emphasis of the National Guilds League was almost entirely on that "status of man as man" which the Malvern Report adduces as demanding changes "in the managerial framework of industry". The League practically ignored any claim of capital to share in control. It envisaged rather that state of affairs which Lord Milner desiderated when he said that in a natural order of things labour would hire capital, not capital labour. In taking up this attitude it was interpreting the bitter resentment of the more class-conscious minds among the workers against their status as mere "hands", or "cogs in the machine". It is significant that this resentment was and is felt not only in the abstract, or because of the contrast between the facts of working life and the flattering words addressed to "free and independent electors" or to alleged heroes whose world should be made fit for them, though both these things counted, but there is also a quite concrete cause of anger found in the fact that men are forced to do work they know to be bad, and have no say in the matter. That classic expression of a workman's

[1] Quoted in op. cit., p. 286, from *Ways and Means* of February 21st, 1920.

wrath and despair, Robert Tressall's *Ragged-Trousered Philanthropists*, is nowhere more poignant than in its description of the sacking of the man who would work too well—who "knew quite well that the foreman objected to any but very large holes or cracks being stopped, and yet somehow or other he could not scamp the work to the extent he was ordered to"; could not bring himself to say with the others "we can't 'elp ourselves, not you nor me either." "Don't you buy a house on the —— Estate," one man was heard to say to another lately. "You put your finger against the walls anywhere, and—it'll go through. *I had to help build 'em, and I know.*" This same resentment has expressed itself more widely than ever in the last two years or so, when the war-motive has made men more than usually critical of knaveries and stupidities forced upon them by their employers. "Criticisms are made," writes a shop steward, "on the score of faulty production methods and hindrances, and are always 100 per cent well-informed." The 100 per cent estimate may be exaggerated, but it is an indication how the men feel about the situation. It is far removed from a mere concern with collective bargaining about wages and conditions. It provides the psychological basis, on the workers' side, for a new guild system.

From this side, too, the necessary changes in structure are in process of formation. In the engineering trades at least, the Works Committees, long fought against by employers and trade union bureaucracies alike, have in the last year or two fully established themselves. They are based on the shop stewards, elected by the members of a particular union working in a particular factory. The job of the steward is thus to look after the interests of his own section within his own works. The movement developed as a reaction against what was felt to be undue centralisation in trade union action. But the Works Committee goes further. It is usually constituted as a conference of the stewards of all the various unions having members in the factory, so that it represents the workers as a whole. It elects its own officers. Under war conditions it represents not only the men's grievances but their criticisms and suggestions about methods of production, and it feels itself a real power in the land.[1] The Trades Union Council has at last been obliged to recognise and even to promote it. "The line of demarcation between the functions of the workers and managerial control" too often seems "an impassable barrier", a member of the T.U.C. Executive told

---

[1] The *Christian Democrat* of February, 1942, has two interesting articles by two members of the movement, describing its aims and methods. "A well-organised factory committee is a real power," writes one of them. "This has been shown by the notice Lord Beaverbrook takes of them, even sacking works managements on their advice." The tables turned indeed!

a South Wales delegates' conference lately; "on the other hand enlightened managements have gone over the line of demarcation, and in many of the workshops in England, Wales and Scotland shop committees have been established, weekly consultations take place, ideas are tried out, and production has gone up." The T.U.C. intended to promote the generalisation of this scheme, and was urging it upon the Cabinet.[1]

It is worth while to quote further two or three testimonies to the sense of liberation on the one hand, and increase of efficiency on the other, which ensue on adoption of the principle of labour's right to share in control. Not least interesting among these is the too-little known Appendix to the Master of Balliol's book *Christianity and Economics*,[2] on the organisation of labour in the Army in France during the war of 1914–18. Dr. Lindsay was a member of the Directorate of Labour, which had charge of the Labour Corps on which all Army Departments drew, and he tells how the Directors became concerned to find a substitute for the ordinary economic incentives to efficiency. They first tried the development of *esprit de corps* by forming the men into companies which were always employed as units, and encouraging them to keep records of their performances. This worked. Next they improved on it by allotting to these units such and such a task of work, leaving to them certain responsibilities for the method of performing it, and allowing the men to take advantage of any time saved. This worked still better. Then came

the third method, the most suggestive and also the most fruitful of the three. It consisted in laying down that the technical services should state, not how many men they wanted, but what work they wanted done, and that the responsibility for the work and for contriving how most efficiently to do it was laid upon the labour company. . . . How they did it, what intervals of rest they took, how they arranged their squads, was their affair. They were not living tools, but men assigned a responsible task and given scope to do it. The results of this method in increased production were extraordinary. . . . In tasks which, when working under the orders of the technical services, they had found only monotonous routine, there was abundant room for thought, for contrivance, initiative, and experiment. . . . They had scope to decide on matters which their daily experience had led them to understand. To be given that is to be given what a man wants for his work.

Again, take the argument of a Trade Unionist in New Zealand.[3] "At present we have political democracy, the citizen can decide

---

[1] See *The Times* of February 11th, 1942.
[2] *Christianity and Economics*, by A. D. Lindsay, pp. 155–77.
[3] W. N. Pharazyn, Pamphlet No. 11 of the Employee Partnership Institute, 1941. A reprint of a broadcast talk given in New Zealand.

who is to rule the country, but the citizen as a wage-earner has no voice as to how his job, from which he secures his living, is to be administered. . . . The course which is surely the one we ought to follow is the extension of political democracy by increasing the responsibility and share in production of the wage-worker until he realises that the administration and discipline and forward-planning of production is his own personal affair as well as that of his employer." Or that of a French working man, H. Dubreuil:[1] "Bureaucracy . . . springs from the fact that *pari passu* with the extension of the business no steps are taken to distribute and decentralise responsibility. . . . The wage system, so far from being a formula of association, is one of antagonism. . . . The need of every man is the need of self-expression, the need more or less consciously felt of creating something of one's own, of achieving some form of independence." M. Dubreuil gives it as a matter of experience that this need can be met by breaking up the labour force in a factory into groups such as can undertake collective contracts, allowing them freely to recruit their own members, to choose their own leaders and organisation, and to distribute their joint earnings among themselves. "When these principles of autonomy, responsibility and initiative were applied to an enterprise in which the author worked, immediately waste was eliminated, interest quickened, rewards improved, human relations sweetened."

Finally, returning to this country, let us quote first the one-time famous Melchett-Turner Report of 1927, and then the letter of a company director in *The Times* of January 6th of this year. The Melchett-Turner Report, representing a conference between an important group of employers and representatives of the T.U.C., declared that "industrial reconstruction can be undertaken only in conjunction with and with the co-operation of those entitled and empowered to speak for organised labour." "Many of us," writes Mr. E. H. Gilpin, of the Westwood Works, Peterborough, "hope to see the day when it will be realised that in modern industry there are three partners, the investor, the manager, and the worker; and that when the investor has received a rent for the use of his capital, commensurate with the risks run, the equity of the business should belong to those actively engaged in its conduct."

Thus we are brought to consider how far the ground is prepared for the Guilds from the side not of labour but of management. The very word reminds us of that highly significant development in the modern industrial structure by which the function of management has been increasingly separated from the function

---

[1] H. Dubreuil, *A Chacun sa Chance*.

of the provision of capital.[1] From the Managing Director down-wards, management in all big industries is as truly hired labour as is the work of the operatives. The salariat is as distinct a class as the proletariat. As such, its interests move often rather with those of the wage-earners than with those of the capitalist; and certainly its interest in the efficient doing of the work, and pride in its quality, is often outraged by the control of merely profit-making considerations. Many of its members are professionally trained, and like all professionals they resent the interference of the unqualified person, based on what to their minds are quite irrelevant considerations. Science, they consider, should obvi-ously take precedence of the mere pursuit of self-interest. They know what it could do in the production of abundance and of quality. If the manual worker resents a sub-human status and the contradiction of his craftsman's instincts, so do the technicians resent the frustration of their trained abilities. This point needs no labouring; it is patent as soon as mentioned. Here again is a strong element in the existing pattern of industry ready and willing to welcome its functionalisation. Its professional associa-tions are ready to be incorporated in the new guilds.

But, after all, when the structure of industry is referred to, it is chiefly understood to mean the type of organisation by which production is directed. The conceptions of wage-labour and specialised management may be included, but attention is focused on "a business", and still more clearly on "the business man". Many small businesses still remain, but the dominant element in the pattern of industry to-day is "big business". Individual firms employ their hundreds or their thousands, and they are knit together in the huge complexes of the trust, the combine or the cartel. Behind these, and dominating them to an increasing extent, stand the banks and the great financing houses. The ultimate purpose is not the production of goods, but the production of profits. Business is not functional, not respon-sible, not organic to the community; its end is within itself—"business is business". Often it may be good business to produce good goods; but often too it is not. A special type of humanity, the business man, is also produced; and he tends to be a hard-faced man. This order of industry fails to satisfy the demands of the Malvern Report that the purpose of work should be the satisfaction of human needs, and that the doing of it should be for the producer a part of "the good life". Nor does it in fact

---

[1] So far as this remains a function. Mr. Keynes does not think that it will long continue to do so. "If I am right in supposing it to be comparatively easy to make capital goods so abundant that the marginal efficiency of capital is zero, this may be the most sensible way of getting rid of many of the most objectionable features of capitalism." J. M. Keynes, *The General Theory of Employment*, p. 221.

even satisfy the economic needs of the community: on the contrary, it admittedly results in periodic crises of increasing violence. It now argues, indeed, that its high degree of organisation will enable it so to plan that in future such disasters may be avoided. But the community can hardly trust to this, in the light of experience, unless the plan rises to the point of setting the public above the private interest. If "business" could do this, it would *ipso facto* cease to be mere "business", and would set about transforming itself into a responsible, functional organisation—in fact, into a Guild system. But more probably it will need to be laid hold of and transformed by the community, as has been done by the Dictator states. It is true, however, as even the very imperfect imposition of responsibility in the interests of war-production has shown, that the elaborate organisation already evolved can be used for the purposes of the community. It has shown, too—if it needed to be shown—that hardness of face is not an unconquerable disease, but that given a cause in which they believe, business men too are willing to subordinate themselves to it. It is not Utopian to hope for a peaceful transition to a New Order in industry.

Indeed, just as we saw that the encroaching control of the trade unions and the professional aspirations of the managerial and technical staff are preparing the way for the incorporation of the workers in a functional order, so the growth of the great modern combines and cartels has created bodies which are crying out to be informed by souls. Society has long been uneasily conscious that to leave in the hands of private interests the enormous economic powers necessarily wielded by such bodies is incompatible with any real political self-government. It has been shocked by revelations of the wars of steel and gold, the politics of oil, and the ghastly cynicism of armaments carpet-baggers. It has at least a confused realisation that if it continues to allow such uncontrolled pursuit of material wealth it is doomed, and deserves its doom. On the other hand the old enthusiasm for collectivisation as a method of control has faded as men experience the smothering growth of bureaucracy, and the choking of political life by the processes of economic planning. Planning, it is recognised, is indeed essential; but it is increasingly clear that the only people who can plan effectively are the people who are doing the job. The responsibility for doing it must be thrown upon their shoulders. But, once again, if that responsibility is socially recognised and enforced, what emerges is a Guild system.

Tentatives in this direction have been made by the creation of such bodies as the B.B.C., which has a corporate conscience and sense of responsibility, though it is far from having an internal corporative structure; the L.P.T.B., which also has a certain recognised public responsibility, and has a highly-developed relationship with the trade unions concerned, though on the other hand it retains more of the profit-making *ethos* than does the B.B.C. The same is perhaps now true of an earlier creation, the Port of London Authority, though that has an evil record in the past. The experiments in control under war conditions have been criticised by doctrinaire collectivists on the very ground that they have laid on industries or on industrial experts the duty of control, instead of imposing it from without. But so far as the criticism has had force it has been because the controls have been assumed to be temporary only, and therefore the industry has inevitably had one eye fixed on conditions in a "return to normality" after the war. On the other hand the experiments are there, and they are leading to widespread speculation as to whether and how far it will be desirable to maintain the structures so created as planning and controlling bodies in a post-war reconstruction. The recent *Times* article *Back to the Guilds*[1] is significant. The writer indeed regards the guilds through eighteenth-century eyes, as selfish limitations on the freedom of the individual rather than through medieval and twentieth-century ones as functional and ethical associations. He may be correct, but on the face of it he seems to be gratuitously cynical in his assumption that it was and is merely hypocrisy when trade associations express a desire for self-regulation in the interest of the maintenance of standards, as in the case which he quotes from a journal of the building trades:

> Is it not high time that builders sought to protect themselves in the same way that architects have done, and try to establish the principle that all directors and managers should be qualified to some degree? No doubt a very large percentage of builders have never passed any examination, but a way could be found of verifying qualification.

The guild structure is primarily designed to unite the members of an industry in the exercise of their function. It exists to defend the standards of the industry, the quality of its products as well as its standard of life. Obviously this defence of standards is not a purely disinterested adventure. Unscrupulous competition may not only hurt the professional pride of the good firm by obliging it to descend to the cheap and shoddy methods of its competitors. It may very well drive it out of business altogether. But the element of professional pride is there as well as that of economic interest; and it is among the highest advantages of the guild that it brings into industry a principle hitherto held to be the

[1] See *The Times* of March 5th, 1942.

standard of "the professions" only, that the work is primary and the pay secondary. The principle of duty towards patient or client is extended to duty towards the customer also. There is no opposition between such a "professionalisation" of an industry and the defence of the standard of life of its members. To demand as well as to pay the just price is part of the defence of a just order of society. When the defence is that of a group on behalf of its members it becomes part of that practical expression of brother-hood which is only to be realised within the comparatively small circle with which a man is anyhow associated. No doubt it is always easy to allow self-defence to degenerate into selfishness; but the guild structure, as compared either with the individualism of free competition or the buccaneering of the cartel, helps instead of hindering the maintanance of an ethical standard.

Assuming that it is the existing cartel or combine or trade association which is made the basis of the new functional corpora-tion or guild, it will readily be seen that the National Guild represents the organised industry as a whole, and is the planning, inspecting and probably the marketing body. But, like the cartel, it will not swallow up, but incorporate, the individual firms in the industry. These too, however, must be transformed according to the guild principle into associations of all those concerned, freely functioning within the plan and standards agreed. As conditions obviously vary from industry to industry, there can be no question of laying down a uniform constitution for them all. The Mining Guild must differ from the Transport Guild, and the Guild of the Clothing Trades from both. It has already been indicated, however, that there should be a National Guilds Council representing all the Guilds. This should as far as possible relieve Parliament from concern with detailed economic legis-lation, and should even share in the determination of general economic policy.[1]

A question which may well be raised at this point is where ownership will be vested under the new dispensation. For legal purposes doubtless companies will be registered then as now as the legal owners. But the sociological question differs from that which will satisfy jurisprudence. In the companies or firms to be organised on Guild principles, everyone concerned, not the contributors of capital only, would share in the ownership. An interesting attempt to work out a technique for estimating

[1] The National Guildsmen of 1910–20 tried to bring the professional and cultural associations into the National Guilds Council, and this procedure has been followed in the Italian organisation. But in fact this contradicts the functional principle. The suggestion in Dr. Temple's "Penguin" is better: that there should be at least two Func-tional Councils, one for Education as well as one for Industry (*Christianity and Social Order*, p. 81).

"Labour shares" in the property has been made by a New Zealand employer, Mr. Valder, and embodied in a permissive Act of Parliament in that home of social experiment. Whether by that method or another, it is of the essence of the Guild idea that every recognised worker in the industry is a member of the guild, and as such shares not only in its government but in its profits, and in the determination of their distribution. Capital (so long as investment from without remains necessary[1]) will be entitled to its agreed interest, management and labour to their agreed pay. Provision will be made for reserves, and for such pensions and allowances (perhaps including family allowances) as the Guild may have instituted. What remains is available for dividend to all members according to their calculated shares. It is an important Guild principle that a man remains on the pay-roll so long as he is regarded as being on the strength of the concern, even if temporarily unemployed. Should it become necessary permanently to reduce the numbers employed beyond what can be done by refraining from filling up vacancies, those displaced, as shareholders in the concern, still retain their claim to dividend. But this claim should be subject to amortisation in order to prevent government by the dead hand.[2] In this way— and it seems the only way open under modern conditions of industry—the claim of the Distributists is met, that every man should have a right of property in the business in which he spends his life. With that he gets some degree of the security and responsibility which go with property; and the natural equity which sees the right to property as arising out of the appropriation of the gifts of nature by means of labour is satisfied.

Would the Guild system, then, still leave industry as a profit-making concern, dependent on the motive of gain? Does it fail to meet all those impassioned protests which have been made against the basing of society on acquisitiveness? Did not the Malvern Conference commit itself, *nemine contradicente*, to the propositions, first,

> That the maintenance of that part of the structure of our society, by which the ultimate ownership of the principal industrial resources of the community can be vested in the hands of private ownership, can be such a stumbling-block as may make it harder for men to live Christian lives.

and secondly, that

[1] Apart from the speculation of Mr. J. M. Keynes quoted above, it is a fact that a large and increasing proportion of industrial capital is now provided out of a company's own profits.

[2] Similar amortisation may probably be applied to capital investments. Cp. the interesting proposals in Dr. Temple's *Christianity and Social Order*, p. 82.

While these resources can be so owned, men will strive for their ownership for themselves. As a consequence, a way of life founded on the supremacy of the economic motive will remain, which is contrary to God's plan for mankind.[1]

Professor Alfred Cobban has lately written a book[2] with the object of proving that almost all the ills from which our civilisation suffers are due to an obsession of the political mind of the last three centuries by an idea which corresponds to nothing in political reality, viz. absolute sovereignty—the sovereign monarch, the sovereign state, the sovereign people. It would be quite possible to write a similar book tracing most of our ills to obsession by a somewhat similar idea which also corresponds to nothing existent, absolute property. Property is in fact a bundle of rights, the contents of which differ at different times and according to the different things over which the rights exist. When the Malvern Report speaks of the "ultimate ownership of industrial resources" as being vested in private ownership, it is perhaps forgetting the bitter protests made throughout the nineteenth century against interference with the rights of property by the whole developing complex of protective legislation and equalising taxation. It is doubtful whether ownership by joint stock companies can properly called be private ownership: Sir Richard Acland himself seems doubtful about it when he remarks that his wife "owns part of the Antwerp waterworks. My grandmother owns part of the Argentine railway system."[3] What rights of property could they exercise over these things? Purely and solely that of drawing income from them. This is indeed one, but only one, in any proper bundle of rights of ownership—which rights, like any other rights, ought to imply duties or responsibilities as their obverse. It is the separation of ownership from responsibility, from function, that is the real quarrel which ethics has with the existing system. Another aspect of the same quarrel is the divorce of the great majority of the citizens from any property at all in the things they work with or produce. It is because property evokes responsible action, as well as a contented mind, that Christian tradition, as summarised by St. Thomas Aquinas,[4] approves it as necessary in this imperfect world. In our particular world of large-scale industry, it seems to be only by allocation of rights of property through a guild system that such functional yet personal property can be restored to the mass of men. With property inevitably goes the right to make profit out of it; but a common profit made by common work and distributed by

[1] *The Life of the Church and the Order of Society*, p. 8.
[2] *The Crisis of Civilization*, by Alfred Cobban.
[3] *Unser Kampf*, by Sir Richard Acland, pp. 43 f.
[4] See e.g. the quotation in Dr. Temple's *Christianity and Social Order*, p. 28.

common agreement. Such profit is poles apart from the profit drawn by the capitalist system from the labour of the wage-earner.[1] Further, it is not merely cynical but unreal to disregard the difference of *ethos* created by the fact that the guild is chartered by the State to perform a certain service to the community. Under capitalism the service of production is incidental to the pursuit of profit. In the professions, and in the Guild idea, the service is primary and the profit secondary. It may be true that the "hard-faced men" of the capitalist system will be likely to carry over the acquisitive mind of the old order into the new, and to strive to make the new Guild only the old Cartel writ large. But there are also numbers of men of goodwill and men with uneasy consciences, as well as men with definitely Christian aspirations, among existing employers and owners, who are already desirous to see a new and better order. There are also always the young; and in these a Guild order will train and not smother their finer instincts.

It was no accident that the industrial system of medieval Christendom was a Guild system, organic to the community— at that time naturally to the municipality, and closely related also to the Church, its worship and its principles of morality. It was part of that conception of society as *communitas communitatum*, a fellowship of fellowships, which as that great historian, Dr. Figgis, taught was a natural and necessary outcome of the existence of the Church itself, a body independent of the State, though not unrelated to it. It is hard to see in what other terms the Church to-day can conceive the fit relation of industry to that new Christendom for which it is surely her privilege and duty to-day to strive hopefully.

---

[1] It is true that the original Guildsmen were stern prophets of equality, and while admitting that Guild was likely to differ from Guild in income, contemplated the return of all surpluses to the National Guilds Council for redistribution, or to the State in relief of taxation. But I do not find this advocated to-day, and the doctrine of property is gradually being clarified.

SOCIALISM THE ONLY WAY TO DEMOCRACY

By Sidney Dark

I AM not sure that, much as they have been discussed, it is realised how clear the Findings of the Malvern Conference are in condemnation of monopoly capitalism. Here are the more important statements:

"The Church can point to those features of our existing society which, while they can never prevent individual men and women from becoming Christian, are contrary to divine justice, and act as stumbling-blocks, making it harder for men to live Christian lives.

"In our present situation we believe that the maintenance of that part of the structure of our society, by which the ultimate ownership of the principal industrial resources of the community can be vested in the hands of private owners, may be such a stumbling-block. On the one hand it may deprive the poorest members of the community of the essentials of life. On the other, while these resources can be so owned, men will strive for their ownership for themselves. As a consequence, a way of life founded on the supremacy of the economic motive will remain, which is contrary to God's plan for mankind. . . .

"It is a traditional doctrine of Christendom that property is necessary to fulness of personal life; all citizens should be enabled to hold such property as contributes to moral independence and spiritual freedom without impairing that of others; but where the rights of property conflict with the establishment of social justice or the general social welfare, those rights should be over-ridden, modified, or, if need be, abolished.

"The proper purpose of work is the satisfaction of human needs; hence, Christian doctrine has insisted that production exists for consumption; but man is personal in all his activities and should find in the work of production a sphere of true human activity, and the doing of it should be for the producer a part of the 'good life' and not only his way of earning a livelihood.

"The existing industrial order, with the acquisitive temper characteristic of our society, tends to recklessness and sacrilege in the treatment of natural resources. It has led to the impoverishment of the agricultural community, and is largely responsible for the problem of the 'mass man', who is conscious of no status, spiritual or social, who is a mere item in the machinery of production, and who easily develops the herd psychology, which is automatically responsive to skilful propaganda."

The word "may" in the second paragraph is unfortunate. It, indeed, suggests a contradiction with the other statements. It is a matter of common knowledge that monopoly capitalism not only "may" deprive the poorer members of the community of the essentials of life, but that, for generations, it has deprived them of those essentials.

The Findings go on to declare that to a large extent production is carried on not to supply the consumer with goods but to bring profits to the producer ("to a large extent" should be "primarily"); that the concern for monetary gain is the source of unemployment at home and dangerous competition for markets abroad; that the rights of labour must be recognised as in principle equal to those of capital in the control of industry, and that in international trade a genuine interchange of mutually needed commodities must take the place of a struggle for a so-called favourable balance. And the Findings add that the objective of social reconstruction should be: "The restoration of man's economic activity to its proper place as the servant of his whole personal life; and the expression of his status in the natural world as a child of God for whom Christ died."

In his *Christianity and Social Order*, which may be regarded as the sequel to Malvern, the Archbishop of Canterbury has laid down a six-fold objective:

(1) "Every child should find itself a member of a family housed with decency and dignity so that it may grow up as a member of that basic community in a happy fellowship unspoilt by underfeeding or overcrowding, by dirty and drab surroundings, or by mechanical monotony of environment."

(2) "Every child should have the opportunity of an education till years of maturity, so planned as to allow for his peculiar aptitudes and make possible their full development. This education should throughout be inspired by faith in God and find its focus in worship."

(3) "Every citizen should be secure in possession of such income as will enable him to maintain a home and bring up children in such conditions as are described in paragraph 1 above."

(4) "Every citizen should have a voice in the conduct of the business or industry which is carried on by means of his labour and the satisfaction of knowing that his labour is directed to the wellbeing of the community."

(5) "Every citizen should have sufficient daily leisure, with two days of rest in seven, and if an employee, an annual holiday with pay, to enable him to enjoy a full personal life with such interests and activities as his tasks and talents may direct."

(6) "Every citizen should have assured liberty in the forms of freedom of worship, of speech, of assembly, and of association for special purposes."

It has been necessary for me to set out these authoritative statements of the immediate demands of the Christian social reformer because it is the purpose of this essay to urge what is, I believe, the only possible way by which the desired ends may be attained.

My own position is perfectly clear. I am a Social Democrat. I agree with a recent statement of Mr. Hayim Greenberg in *Left News* that "democracy is the ultimate goal; and socialism is, under modern industrial conditions, the practical means for the attainment of this goal of individual worth and equality." I agree, too, with the contention of the authors of *U.S.S.R.: Its Significance for the West* that "an increase in total individual liberty it not only compatible with, but dependent on an increase in the compulsory powers of the State." When I was very young, I became a Socialist mainly from reading William Morris's *News from Nowhere* and Robert Blatchford's *Merrie England*, and from listening to Socialist speeches at the Salle Wagram in Paris and at Kelmscott House at Hammersmith. My revolt against the existing order was because it made life for the majority ugly and frustrated. From the *Fabian Essays* I learned that it was wasteful and stupid; from Scott Holland I learned that it was wicked, an offence to Almighty God.

As I grew older, I became more and more afraid of the malign influence of Puritanism. I did not cease to believe that, by Parliamentary enactments, social and economic changes could be effected that would make the lives of the majority happier and fuller, but I saw in the influence of the Webbs, the heirs of the Puritan tradition, and in the dominating position in the Labour Party of a middle-class Puritan like Philip Snowden the danger of a planned society in which the individual would be no more than an efficient cog in a machine, and in which there would be no more cakes and ale, since they might impair individual efficiency. My views at this time are set out at length in the introduction to my novel, *The Man Who Would Not Be King* which I have recently reprinted in my *Not Such a Bad Life*.

In the years between the wars, it became more and more obvious that the power of money was growing more and more predominant and more and more mischievous. The slump at the end of the twenties was clearly due to the juggling of the money markets; the consequent cuts in the social services were evidence both of the selfishness of the possessing classes and of the comparative impotence of organised labour resulting from the failure of the general strike in 1926. Unemployment was accepted as inevitable; Parliament was controlled by second rate men with a definite class outlook. Everywhere one saw want and waste and the more observant began to anticipate war. The old order had broken down. It was dying from its own ineptitude and not from the attacks of the people who suffered most from it. Long before the end of 1939 it was evident that the destruction or perhaps the radical modification of monopoly capitalism was vital not only for the securing of a better life for the majority but to preserve the general standard of living that had been attained. Such freedom as the majority possessed was of little value in the existing conditions of insecurity, and I became as convinced as I had been, years before, that Socialism was the only system in which civilisation could be safeguarded and developed.

The war has cleared the air as it has destroyed many of the slums. Capitalism is down and out, and, with it, all its trimmings. As the latest Fabian Society manifesto says: "There has been no such holocaust of established institutions since the advent of the Dark Ages; nay, even then much less of the human race was shaken by the collapse of the ancient empires than is being shaken to-day."

There is now no possibility of patching up, or of the modificatoins suggested in the Malvern Findings. Malvern wants decent and dignified homes for all the people. Malvern wants a revival of agriculture for the maximum production of food while securing good wages for the country worker and a just price for the farmer. But homes for the people cannot be built, the land cannot be adequately tilled, the labourer and the farmer cannot be properly paid so long as the community recognises the private ownership of land. If the landlord is allowed to go on imposing his private taxes, the community simply will not be able to find the money for the houses, for the land development or for the workers' wages. This is not fundamentally a question of right or wrong; it is one of the hard facts of the times that, in the impoverished post-war world, the community will not be able to afford the landlord. He will be an anachronistic nuisance.

He will have to go and there will be no money with which "to buy him out". Expropriation, practically without compensation, will be demanded by both the Malvern principles and by common sense. Unless this is accepted it is a sheer waste of time to plan the building of new and fair towns or to discuss how the production of the land may be stimulated.

Similarly with coal mines, if the nation is to have the heating, the lighting and the power necessary for its domestic and industrial life, and, if the miners are to have tolerable wages, there must be no more royalties from the mines, and no more dividends for the mine owners. Christians must make up their minds who is to benefit, the few or the many. One class or the other must suffer. Exactly the same thing applies to the means of transport and all the public services.

There is considerable attraction in the ideal of Mr. De Valera of a self-supporting community feeding itself, producing its own necessities and dependent on nothing essential from other nations. But, so far as this country is concerned, this is the fantastic dream of the medievalists who yearn for the return of the Maypole, the handloom and spade agriculture. If every acre of the country were cultivated to the fullest possible advantage, the present population could not be fed without exports even as inadequately as it was fed before the war. Without vast imports of raw material, the industrial machine could not produce the bare necessities of life for that population. We must import to live; we must export to be able to import.

Before the war, exports were progressively declining. Great Britain was no longer the factory of the world. After the war it will be tremendously difficult to regain even the pre-war markets, and it has to be remembered that the overseas credits, accumulated in the good times, which have enabled foreign buying to go on, will have been exhausted by the war purchases.

Somehow or the other we must contrive to produce goods that other peoples will want to buy at prices that they can afford to pay. The double problem will be to improve quality and to reduce costs. This will mean nation-wide planning and the elimination of all avoidable charges. The type of goods to be produced must no longer be determined by the private capitalist with his desire for quick private profits but by consideration for the permanent national well-being. It will have to be accepted that a nation, with a comparatively high standard of comfort, cannot compete in the manufacture of cheap goods that can just as well be produced by cheap foreign labour. Our workers are still characterised by a high degree of skill and that skill will be best employed in turning out goods of the highest possible quality. We have been pushed out of the shoddy market. Perhaps we should thank God that we can never push our way back into it.

Just as the fertility of the land must be exploited scientifically, so the output of the factories must be directed by foresight and judgment. Competition between factory and factory must be eliminated. Experts, managers, and workers must combine to make to sell so that the nations can and will buy. It is notorious that markets have been lost by the pig-headed stupidity of private industrialists who have endeavoured to sell not what the foreigner wants but what he was convinced that he ought to want. We shall not be able to afford that sort of stupidity in the future. It is certain that a National Manufacturing and Marketing Board would make blunders but it could not possibly make more blunders than the private capitalist has made.

It would be merely futile to suggest that the breakdown of the capitalist system has been due to the stupidity of the capitalist. The house has tumbled to pieces not because the builders have lacked skill but because it was built on the sands of an essentially unrighteous economic objective. The new house will have the solid foundation of righteousness and common sense.

If there is to be Malvern's "genuine interchange of mutually needed commodities sufficient to meet this country's reasonable demands", there must be on the one hand the stimulation of buying by the raising of the standard of living in the backward countries and the rigorous restriction of imports by the State. Nothing should be shipped from abroad that can only be bought by the few. If the general standard of comfort is to be retained, with the possibility that it may be raised, luxuries will have to disappear from the national economy.

The first of these conditions implies that prosperity must be internationally shared if it is to be nationally enjoyed. The great majority of the peoples on this earth are still miserably poor, with the meagrest purchasing power. For the common good they must be helped to develop their natural resources, and to secure far better living conditions.

Imperialist capitalism has "developed" backward countries with the one idea of obtaining the greatest return for the money that it has invested and with practically no regard for the "subject peoples". British capitalism, for example, has done very well out of India. It has received full measure, pressed down and running over, for "opening up" the country. But the people of India have not done very well, and after 150 years they are for the most part just not starving. The same thing is true of Malaya and of the African colonies.

The political consequences have been that the Malayans were indifferent as to whether they were to be ruled by Britons or by Japanese, that a considerable proportion of the Burmese welcomed the Japanese, and that it has been impossible to organise united Indian action to resist a threatened Japanese invasion. Economically, Imperialist capitalism has kept down the economic level of the "subject people" so that they have only been the potential buyers of very small quantities of the cheapest goods.

I am assuming that Russia will remain a Socialist state and that Socialism will be established in Western Europe with the consequent passing of the control of credit from private to public hands. That would inevitably lead to the establishment of an International Economic Council which, in consultation with the national councils and constantly considering the various local needs, would direct and regulate international exchanges of commodities and make advances for local developments from an international fund. This is not in the least Utopian or unpracticable. It is much what is being done now that the Allied nations may win the war.

I have said that reduction of cost is also essential for the foreign trade without which this country can hardly live. Again common sense dictates that the first economy should be the ceasing of a toll on industry imposed by people who give back to the community nothing in return. The complete socialisation of industry at once is not a practical proposal, and I accept the Fabian Society's suggestion that there are four immediate essentials, the control of capital and credit for production, the control of land, the control of the import and export trade and the control of transport and of the supply of fuel and power. If these were secured, production and distribution generally would no longer be dominated by the private profit seeking motive that Malvern condemned.

The Fabian Society agrees with Dr. Temple, and apparently with Sir Richard Acland, that "we must be content for the time being to regulate the profit system rather than to abolish it", the profit system, that is, in the small industries. It has to be remembered (I myself have been apt to forget it) that even to-day with the tendency towards combines, the majority of businesses, both manufacturing and distributive, are comparatively small affairs, and the returns from a business, that a man owns and himself directs may be fairly regarded as wages rather than as profits. I confess that I regard the small shopkeeper as a rather pathetic survival, struggling with overheads and bad debts and frequently going bankrupt after years of the struggle. There can be no question that on the whole the chain stores sell better goods at a lower price. Moreover, as was pointed out long ago, the well organised combines can be easily taken over by the community when the time is ripe. But for a while the small business will probably remain.

Since the reduction of cost in both production and distribution of commodities for export and for home consumption is so necessary, the profits, now distributed among the shareholders in concerns that will be left in private ownership, will have to be limited by law, and the Archbishop of Canterbury has made the admirable suggestion that after cent per cent has been paid on the investment, no more interest should be received.

So far I have put the case for Socialism on utilitarian grounds. Competitive capitalism has broken down. The State control of finance and industry is already established in the greater part of Europe, and as a war time necessity in Great Britain. It must continue here unless we are prepared for economic and industrial chaos, and I am convinced that sooner or later (probably later) it will be established in the United States. But the State control of industry is not Socialism, as I understand it, and it certainly need not be democratic because no rational State can tolerate the waste that capitalism has at times encouraged for its own ends; it may establish equality of opportunity in order that it may get the best possible service from its citizens; it may see to it that the people live in conditions that make for health and efficiency; and it may provide a plentiful supply of circuses as well as of bread. This country may indeed become a sort of benevolent Fascist State, with economic security and modified equality of opportunity for the majority, and with the continuance of the privileged if considerably impoverished minority, who would retain political and economic control. In such an economy, there might well be the intelligent direction of imports and exports that I have urged, and a large reduction in the cost of production and distribution, but the luxury subsistence of the *rentiers* would make it impossible for the genuine standard of living to be raised, and indeed it is most unlikely that it could be maintained at the present level. Further, as has been made clear in both Germany and Russia, the effectiveness of such a system depends on its success in compelling complete obedience from the majority. Personal freedom would cease to exist.

Writing of Christian Ethics and Christian Politics in his *Christianity and Social Order*, the Archbishop of Canterbury says:

"The primary principle of Christian Ethics and Christian Politics must be respect for every person simply as a person. If each man and woman is a child of God, whom God loves and for whom Christ died, then there is in each a worth absolutely independent of all usefulness to society. The person is primary, not the society; the States exists for the citizen, not the citizen for the State. The first aim of social progress must be to give the fullest possible scope for the exercise of all powers and qualities which are distinctly personal; and of these the most fundamental is deliberate choice."

Any society in which personal freedom is destroyed or unduly restricted, is to be condemned from the Christian point of view. Fascism, however benevolent it may be, must affect this freedom and is therefore intolerable to the Christian. And Fascism is the only alternative to Socialism. Canon Demant has said, among other odd and surprising things that Fascism is "the contemporary form of Socialism". Actually it is the last resort of capitalism, the attempt to retain the existence of the privileged minority, in the planned economic order, which world developments have made inevitable. As Franz Bortenau says in a recent number of *Horizon*: "The story of Fascism is the story of Conservatives driven into revolution—and a fierce and sweeping sort of revolution—unknowingly and much against their instincts."

In modern conditions, Socialism alone can preserve freedom and make it real and inspiring but, before I come to this contention, I would stress that just as Fascism is to be condemned because it destroys freedom so capitalism is primarily to be condemned because it has denied real freedom to the majority. I have summarised the material case against it, its stupidity and its wastefulness, but the moral case is far more important. Because the conviction that capitalism is an offence to Almighty God, so strong in the minds of the Socialists of a generation ago, has been lost, the British Socialist movement has also lost its moral power. On the continent the Socialist parties were impotent to resist the new tyrannies. Here the Labour Party has preferred political opportunism to any sort of conviction. Capitalism has been destroyed but not by the Socialists and, if now they do not put their case far higher than the demand for secure and adequately paid work for all, it will not be Socialism that will follow the old time capitalism. Not only can men not live on bread alone, but they will not spend themselves to fight for bread alone. Man is a moral animal ultimately most interested in moral issues, and Fascism as well as Socialism can promise and has proved that it can provide a full bread basket.

In the old order, children have gone hungry and families have been vilely housed. That has been bad enough. But what has been worse has been the moral degradation resulting from the evil material conditions. The result of the private ownership of the industrial resources of the community has been, Malvern found, to rob the poorest member of the community of the essentials of life, the spiritual as well as the material essentials. In his *A Cornish Childhood*, A. L. Rowse, the brilliant historian, who was born of struggling working-class parents writes with unqualified bitterness of the qualities of the majority (I hate the term "masses"). They are, he says, characterised by "congealed stupidity, childishness, credulity, liability to panic", by "the matchless unimaginativeness, the absence of nerves or mind or sensibility". They are incapable of thinking, and so on.

Mr. Rowse writes with the memory of the unhappiness of an imaginative boy, living in an entirely unsympathetic atmosphere, and it is interesting to compare his attitude to his class (he is careful to claim that he is still a proletarian) with that of Dickens. But if his statement is exaggerated, and I think that it is, it is not to be denied that the prevailing economic conditions have shut away the majority from the knowledge and the enjoyment of the things of the mind and the imagination. In their scurried and meagre schooling they have not been helped to think. In the grind and anxiety of their adult lives, they have had little time and little opportunity to dream. So they have been easily fooled and easily made content and the circumstances, that have made them what they are, have been exploited by the minority to keep them where they are.

But as life has been made less unendurable by the extension of the social services, by better education and by higher wages and shorter working hours, concessions made according to Joseph Chamberlain's doctrine of ransom to keep the people quiet, there has been an increased popular demand for the good and the beautiful in nature, in literature and in art. There has been an immense extension of the area of geniune æsthetic appreciation since Mr. Rowse's childhood in his Cornish village. The people have been shut away from the light. That does not imply that they prefer the darkness.

It may be true, as Mr. Raymond Mortimer has said, that only a tiny proportion of any community will ever be capable "of enjoying the strenuous exercise of the intellect and the imagination". It is a gross injustice that the enjoyment should be the monopoly of a tiny proportion of a tiny class. Moreover for the less gifted there are many gracious things in life, leisure, space, comely surroundings, that make for sweetness and light, all in their way things of the spirit, and they have been the monopoly of the few. The condemnation of capitalism is primarily spiritual. The condemnation of Fascism is primarily spiritual. The case for Socialism must be primarily spiritual if it is to prevail.

In one of his recent books, Hilaire Belloc has declared that greed is the most powerful of human motives, and in his sympathetic *Mission to Moscow*, Mr. Joseph Davies continually repeats that the attempt to create a classless society in Russia has been defeated by human nature. The output of the Soviet factories could only be increased, so Mr. Davies says, by large extra payment to the most industrious and the most expert workers. And the conclusion is that men will only do their best when they are working for themselves and not primarily for the community. Certainly greed has been the main action motive in the old society, and it has been encouraged by the amoral basis of this society.

The Fabian Society at least partly supports Mr. Davies when it asks: "Does anyone seriously suppose that if, in time of peace, the entire body of workers were put on guaranteed time-wages, paid regardless of output, production would not suffer at any rate in the short run?" It probably would, but the temptation to ca' canny would be decreased if the worker knew that idle people were not growing fat on his labour, and surely it will not be impossible to encourage in peace time the same general acceptance of the duty and the privilege of each giving his best for the common good, that is common and natural when the nation is at war. Capitalism has encouraged greed, and I believe that Socialism will encourage the eagerness for effective service first for the personal satisfaction that comes from a job well done, and then from the social satisfaction of being a valuable and consequently an appreciated member of the community.

I do not believe that men will only give their best if they are able to gain for themselves better food, better clothes and a better house than their fellows have. The poet, the artist, and the scientist work for the pure joy of the task, and Eric Gill has insisted that there is no essential spiritual difference between the men of genius and the men of average ability. Would any soldier, however hard up, sell his Victoria Cross? And in a co-operative society the Victoria Cross would be the recognition of effective service in peace. Greed is not the only human action motive. I do not believe that it is the least powerful. I am certain that it is not general, even now.

Attractive as it is on the surface, I cannot believe that the corporatism, explained and advocated so ably in this volume, is either desirable or practical. As I have said earlier in this essay, it was the Anarchist Communism of William Morris that attracted me in my youth but the news that Morris brought to us was in fact news from nowhere. His world of the future was an idealised picture of a world that was dead. Humanity cannot go back. There were many splendid things in the life of the middle ages as there were many cruel and horrid things. The creations of those centuries that remain for us, suggest that the lives of our forefathers must have been more comely and happier than our lives in this machine age. But the machines cannot be scrapped. We have learned that the belief of Herbert Spencer and other Victorians in the inevitability of progress was an illusion. Men have grown neither happier nor better and whether or no they are in the future to have a chance to grow happier and better depends on whether or no they are able to master the machine and not to remain its slaves. Inventions and discoveries have contrived the maiming and killing of men's bodies and the destruction of the freedom of their souls. The task now is to use the machine to add to the completeness of peace rather than to add to the horrors of war, to lighten and not to darken the lives of the majority, which means that the machine must be employed for the benefit of all and not for the enrichment of the few. The Guilds were the eminently Christian institutions of the centuries of the craftsmen. I do not believe that their revival is possible in the complicated industrialism of the century of the machine. The idea is a very jolly dream, but it is just a dream.

The control of industry by councils representing owners, managers, workers, and consumers is obviously possible. It was recommended by Malvern. It has been partially effected to meet the necessities of the war. It may well be the shape of things to come. It is indeed the only alternative to Social Democracy but it is the road to Fascism.

As I understand it, the case against corporatism is again moral and religious. In such a system the individual would be primarily a miner, or a railwayman. His first interests would be class interests. The wider and more inspiring interests of citizenship would be discouraged and would be less influential even than they are now, for now the miner realises than, to obtain better conditions in the pits, he must have the support of the whole of organised labour, with the backing of the nation through its elected representatives in Parliament.

The nation will be as foolish to admit that the miners are the owners of the mines or even part owners as it has been foolish to permit the shareholders in the mining companies to "own" the pits and the coal that comes from them. It may be argued that the representation of the consumers, that is of the nation, on the mining councils would be the admission that production is for consumption and would safeguard the general interests. But I cannot conceive how the consumers' representation could be real and the war expedients confirm this scepticism. The representatives would have to be nominated by the Government and in practice they would be the spokesmen of the class on which a particular government depended for its continuance in office. Generally the consumers to be considered would be the large consumers and the little man with his two or three hundredweights a week would continue to be disregarded.

Further, as the present owners are to be left with their profits, regulated and limited though they would be, and with a considerable voice in the direction, the well-being of the community as a whole might continue to be an entirely secondary consideration in the running of the industry. It is, indeed, conceivable that, if their wages were safeguarded, the miners might on occasion agree to the limiting of production in order to keep up prices. A stronger exclusive class would be created with the power to hold the community to ransom.

I have taken mining as an example because of its pre-eminent importance but the same objection applies to the similar control of any of the major industries. The mines, the railways, the land, should be regarded as the property of the nation, not of the men who work on them, though they have the right to demand from the nation a full, secure and satisfying life in return for their services to the community. The case for common ownership is stated convincingly by Sir Richard Acland, who has dealt with the objection that common ownership must mean red tape, unintelligent bureaucratic tyranny and industrial stagnation. I do not propose to go over the ground again.

I can sum up my case by repeating two contentions. The first is that it is only through Socialism that real democracy can be attained and that therefore the Christian, with his concern for the fullest possible spiritual freedom for the individual, must support Sir Richard Acland's demand for common ownership of the land and certain essential industries as the first step towards a Socialist state. The second contention that I have already elaborated is that without the national control of credit and the control of exports and imports for the general advantage and not for private gain, after-war distress in this country is certain and further wars more than probable.

It is suggested that the appalling muddles of war production are evidence of the inevitable results of the communal control of industry. As a matter of fact the muddles are solely due to the opposing private interests, the hope of the monopolists to secure the old profits when the war is over and to the continuance of both greed and prejudice in high places. Capitalism has entirely failed to adapt itself to novel and threatening conditions. The captains of industry have shown themselves as wanting in resource as the generals and the general staffs. And I am convinced that, in both cases, class interest has shortened vision and prevented understanding.

I believe, and Russia justifies the belief, that with the feeling of comradeship and the zest for efficient public service that will come with Socialism there will be a genuine advance in the average intelligence, and far more satisfactory leadership since the incompetent will no longer be kept in office because he belongs to the moneyed governing caste.

While an increase in individual liberty depends on an increase in the compulsory powers of the State, and real democracy can be created only by Socialism, there is still the possibility that liberty might be curtailed in a Socialistic state. Democracy implies even more than freedom of speech, freedom of association, and freedom to develop one's own personality. It excludes, as G. D. H. Cole has well said, "too much tidiness, too much order, too much having everything taped". Democracy denies the right of the State to attempt to make men good by Act of Parliament. It is the antithesis of Puritanism and it is Christianity in practice. It involves—I am again following Cole—a real sense of comradeship, friendliness, and brotherhood.

It may not be true, as Rousseau believed, that democracy can only exist in a small community but it is certainly true that the democratic spirit must be born and must be cultivated among small groups of people. We are bidden to love our neighbour as ourselves. We are not bidden to love the stranger within our gates as ourselves, since it is not possible to love people whom we do not know. Democracy, therefore, begins with the realisation that my interests are the interests of the man next door and that his interests are mine, and that it is only by agreeing and acting together that our common interests can be safeguarded. This is first realised perhaps in the family, then in the street, and the parish, and the narrow comradeship continually extends. The Trade Union joins the Trade Union Congress, retaining its own peculiar interests but having learned that those interests are similar to those of other workers. The miners need the help of the engineers, and the clerks must stand shoulder to shoulder with the furniture makers. The little groups create the large groups and the parish, instinct with comradeship, is the foundation of a democratic nation.

Dr. Barker regards democracy as government by discussion. But democracy is more than a system of government. It is a spiritual condition. Discussion is, as Professor Laski insists, only the means towards an end, the end being the discovery of the predominant general will. And it is only after this has been determined that the spirit of democracy functions, in securing from the minority a willing submission to the decision of the majority.

Under capitalism the will of the majority has not been and could not be the prevailing force in the direction of public affairs, because of the economic stranglehold on the community of a privileged minority. What Hitler derides as pluto-democracy has been pseudo-democracy. It has been the rule of the few, posing as the rule of the many, who have been rendered comparatively politically impotent by what Jeremy Bentham called "sinister interests", and Dr. Barker's "discussion" has been of small practical value.

It is argued that Lincoln's "government of the people, for the people, by the people" is an unattainable sentimentality, that the majority will always be too concerned with their own personal affairs to be actively politically minded, except at intervals and for a short time, and that, as in Russia, government will remain the monopoly of a keen minority. That must happen unless the nation, as a whole, is democratically trained for an intelligent concern for communal interests, first in small things and then in the greater things.

There might remain the danger of the majority tyrannising over the minority and of refusing to them the right of criticism and of anti-government agitation. That will only be avoided if democracy is a living spiritual force and not a mere opportunist device, if it is realised that freedom for no one is secure unless, within reasonable limits, freedom is granted to all.

Bertrand Russell asserts that security of government is a condition of the freedom of the citizens and that this security depends on peace, majority consent and economic content. The economic content must of course be shared by all; the majority may change its mind from time to time and the colour of the government may change with it; a secure democratic government must be threatened by war. We have learned that war is directly fomented by capitalism and that the manoeuvres of the masters of the money markets create the booms and slumps that are the economic causes of war. Until democracy is established in all the greater nations peace can never be assured. The conclusion is that, as Trotzky believed that Socialism in Russia must be in peril until the whole of Europe at least became Socialist, so democracy cannot be nationally secure until the whole world is democraticised.

Our business is to make our own country a real democracy and then to see to it that the "subject peoples" of the British Empire enjoy exactly the same freedom that we have established for ourselves. As a matter of fact it would be impossible for a democracy to carry on the Imperial rule of other races without the betrayal of its faith. It must accept the assertion that the rule of one people by another is morally wrong and it would at once leave Indians, West Indians, and Africans to work out their own political and economic problems in their own way, with benevolent and properly modest advice, but with no assumption of the right to order or forcefully to interfere.

Immense difficulties will have to be overcome, and there will be many serious setbacks before Social Democracy prevails. If it is the mere dream of the sentimentalist so is Christianity, and it is a mockery for us to pray "Thy will be done on earth as it is in heaven." Humanity is being tortured by hate and lies. John

Strachey rightly declares that hatred and lies can only be overcome by love and truth. The demand therefore for a social order based on love and truth, based that is on the teaching of Christ, comes not from an unworldly sentimentality but from the realistic regard for facts.